AIKIDO
The Complete Basic Techniques

AIKIDO

The Complete Basic Techniques

Gozo Shioda
with Yasuhisa Shioda

TRANSLATED BY **Damian Bayford**

Even when surrounded by 5 opponents, Gozo Shioda could bring his opponents
off balance in the blink of an eye and throw them.

Originally published in Japanese as *Aikido Kihon-waza*
by Aikido Yoshinkai Koho-bu in 1978.

Photos by Hiroshi Kobayashi and Aikido Yoshinkan.

Distributed in the United States by Kodansha America, Inc.,
and in the United Kingdom and continental Europe
by Kodansha Europe, Ltd.

Published by Kodansha International, Ltd.,
17–14 Otowa 1-chome, Bunkyo-ku, Tokyo 112–8652,
and Kodansha America, Inc.

First edition, 2006
06 07 08 09 10 11 12 13 14 15   10 9 8 7 6 5 4 3 2 1

www.kodansha-intl.com

CONTENTS

SHIHO-NAGE 四方投げ ▪ Multi-Directional Throw 32

IKKAJO-OSAE 一ヵ条抑え ▪ First Control 42

NIKAJO-OSAE 二ヵ条抑え ▪ Second Control 70

NIKAJO-SHIME NO KATA 二ヵ条締めの形 ▪ The Various Forms of the Second Control Technique 70

FOREWORD

Aikido is about developing the ability to focus your physical strength. It is the learning of techniques to overcome your opponent by concentrating all your strength into one area of your body, be it your hands, legs, or back. In the same way as a baseball batter who hits the ball with timing and focus will get a hit or a homerun, with a combination of concentration and timing you can perform exceptional throws. Timing comes naturally with continued practice, but to develop physical focus, there are certain Basic Exercises to practice in which you move your arms, legs, and body in unison, enabling you to learn to focus your strength.

There are 6 Basic Exercises (made up of 2 Body Movement Exercises, 2 Body Line Exercises, and 2 Finishing Exercises) that help you to focus your strength when moving in a straight line or in a curve. Moving in a straight line is like the movements used in boxing or Kendo when attacking. Moving in a curve is a circular movement which uses your opponent's momentum. When you have mastered these two ways of moving you will be able to perform an infinite number of throws. 200 of the most essential of these throws are collected here in the Basic Throws section. In addition to the Basic Throws, which are the main focus of this textbook, there is also a short section on Applied Techniques.

In addition to developing your ability to focus, the idea of synchronizing your spirit is also important in Aikido. This is the literal meaning of the Chinese characters Ai (joining together, synchronizing) and Ki (spirit, mind, heart), which are used to make up the word 'Aikido' in Japanese. Synchronizing your spirit means achieving harmony with your opponent, or in other words becoming one with your opponent. Becoming one with your opponent entails becoming selfless, emptying your mind, and letting go of your emotions and ego. When you let go of your emotions, you enter an unrestrained state of mind where nothing disturbs you. In this state of mind your powers of concentration will be at their fullest.

Through Aikido practice, you will gain a continual desire to improve yourself, and you will naturally acquire the spirit and etiquette of martial arts. Furthermore, as Aikido does not involve the excessive use of force, it can be studied by anybody; old and young, men and women alike. Indeed, this can be said to be one of the greatest attractions of Aikido.

When You Train

I think you will discover when you actually try out the techniques that it is difficult to execute them as smoothly as they appear in the textbook. By first practicing the basics in front of a mirror, you will find that your techniques, with time, become more and more effective. If you rely on your arm strength alone, your movements will become dull, and your posture will suffer. I urge you, therefore, to try as much as possible not to rely on your arm strength, but to move your whole body. In Aikido it is vitally important to practice thoroughly, paying attention to small details. Pay attention to where you are looking, the direction your toes are pointing in, and the form of your hands. Keep your back straight, and your knees flexible, and strive to keep your balance. When you practice with an opponent (partner), it is also important to keep the correct spacing between yourselves. Remember that not only the techniques but also the way you approach your training is important. Empty your mind of your emotions and concentrate solely on the techniques.

About this Textbook

This book is a translation of an updated version of an in-house textbook that was originally made some thirty years ago and was not for sale to the public. In the new textbook, some phrases and photographs have been revised and updated, and a section on Practical Application has been added. This textbook includes a wealth of valuable information on the techniques of my father Gozo Shioda, famous as the leading figure in the world of Aikido. Furthermore, as it includes almost all of the most important basic throws, I believe it is valuable both as a study aid to practice and as a collection of reference material. It is my hope that many people will use this textbook as a reference as they practice Aikido that is both faithful to the basics and rich in content.

Yasuhisa Shioda

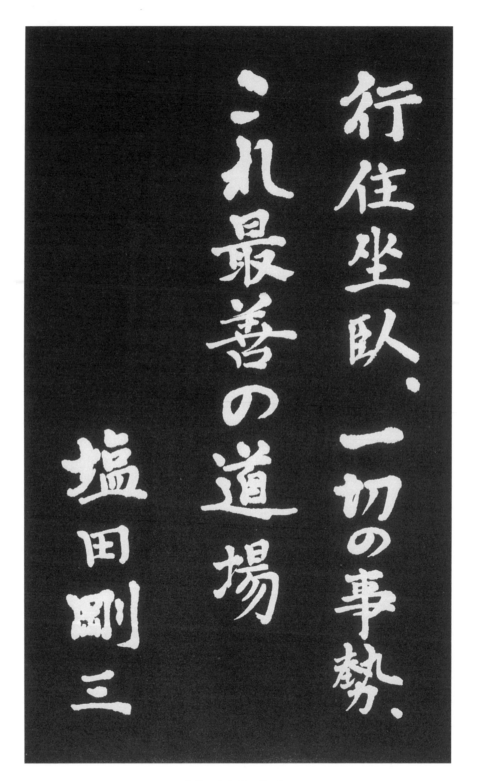

Calligraphy by Gozo Shioda:
"The way you conduct yourself everyday in the ever-changing world is the ultimate training."

CHAPTER 1

THE BASICS 基礎

KIHON SHISEI 基本姿勢
Basic Posture

KAMAE 構え
Stance

The basic Aikido stance is side on, and can be left or right foot forward. The Aikido stance is the necessary starting point for practicing all the techniques that follow in this book for both you and your opponent. It is also the physical expression of your state of mind. The perfect stance is one that has to come without thinking, without trying. In other words, it has to come naturally. You will have to practice over and over again in order to achieve an ideal stance, mentally and physically. With one foot forward and one foot back, the Aikido stance is suited to both defense and attack.

① ②

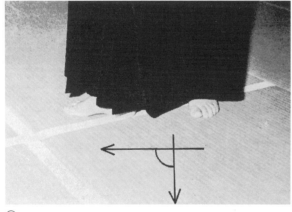

③

④

MIGI HANMI 右半身
(Right-Handed) Basic Stance

①② Stand right foot forward, as though you are holding a sword aimed at your opponent's face.

③ Your feet should be open, which means that your toes should be facing slightly outward. Stand with your feet a foot and a half apart, which is the best distance for stability and the easiest for moving forward and backward. This footing will enable you to manage the turning movements unique to Aikido more easily and will give your body a strong triangular base. Your weight should be distributed 60% over your front foot.

④ Hold your right arm out at chest level, with your elbow extended, as though you are holding a sword's curved blade. Your left hand should be held a few inches in front of your stomach. Open and spread the fingers of both hands, pointing them at your opponent. You should look your opponent in the eyes, without losing sight of his body as a whole. Your attention should not be focused only on your opponent; be aware of all that is around you.

IMPORTANT POINTS

- Do not stick your head out in an attempt to show you are focused forward.
- Keep your back and waist straight.
- Do not tense your shoulders or allow your upper body to become stiff.
- Open your fingers.
- Do not let your knees become stiff, and concentrate on putting your strength into the big toe on both feet.
- Look your opponent squarely in the eyes.

AI HANMI 相半身
Same-Handed Stance

⑤ Both you and your opponent face each other, adopting the same-handed stance. (In other words both of you are right foot forward or both left foot forward.)

GYAKU HANMI 逆半身
Opposite-Handed Stance

⑥ This is when you and you opponent adopt the basic stance with the opposite foot forward. (In other words you are right foot forward and your opponent left foot forward.)

MA-AI 間合
Spacing

Spacing refers to the distance you set between you and your opponent for defense or attack. The closer you are to your opponent, the easier it is to attack, and the more difficult it is to defend. The further you are from your opponent, the easier it is to defend, and the more difficult it is to attack. Though choosing the best spacing for each situation is important, for Aikido training you generally stand just far apart enough from your opponent so that even if both of you stretch out your arms or legs you can't quite touch. This distance, about 1.8 meters, is called "normal spacing."

SHITE AND UKE 仕手と受
You and Your Opponent

In Aikido training all moves are practiced so that the person performing the throw and the person being thrown are determined beforehand. Throws are performed with the co-operation of the person being thrown. In Japanese the person performing the throw is called Shite, and the person who ends up being thrown is called Uke. In the terminology of this book the one doing the throwing is "you," and the one being thrown is called "your opponent." However, as all moves and exercises are practiced in co-operation, "your opponent" may also be thought of as "your partner."

⑤

⑥

KIHON DOSA 基本動作
Basic Exercises

Here you will learn the basics of how to move your arms, legs, and body as a necessary preparation for practicing throws. These basic exercises can be practiced alone or with a partner, though it is best to practice them by yourself first, before practicing with a partner. However, as these basic movements, which are short on variation, are apt to become more like a gymnastics exercise and lose their original form as a martial art, they should be practiced with great care. Here the exercises are explained as practiced with a partner, leaving out the explanation of the exercises when practiced alone.

TAI NO HENKO 体の変更
Body Movement Exercise

Although there is a great number and variety of moves in Aikido, in principle there are only two types of movement—where you turn your body, and when you push forward. In Aikido the golden rule is: If you are pushed, turn. If you are pulled, go forward in a curve.

TAI NO HENKO 1 体の変更 1（引かれた場合）
Body Movement Exercise Type 1 (When pulled)

This is a basic exercise to help you use your opponent's strength when you are pulled, so that combined with good timing you can move forward, make your opponent powerless, and leave yourself in a strong and stable position. It is the most basic form of the technique, special to Aikido, where you use the whole of your whole body to push your opponent. This technique comes into many of the moves you will learn hereafter.

① Stand facing your opponent. Both you and your opponent stand in the basic Aikido stance, right foot forward. Your opponent grasps your left wrist with his right hand and pulls. Make sure your fingers are spread open strongly, and be prepared so that you can make any kind of action. The fingers of your opponent's left hand should also be spread conforming to the basic stance position.

② Slide your left foot forward in a slight curve without lifting your toes off the floor to a position two thirds of the way between your opponent's feet. Put your weight strongly onto your left foot and brace yourself with your right leg, pushing your right hip forward, making the lower half of your body into a strong base.

③ Using your opponent's pull, move your left hand forward, palm up and without bending your elbow, starting right and moving up leftward, aiming for the top of your opponent's left shoulder. Your right hand should shadow the movement of the left hand, starting right, and ending up as though cutting across your opponent's stomach.

④ When moving forward, the toes of the left foot should face outward. The right foot should be at a right angle to your left foot, making a "T" shape. Your left knee should be bent and go beyond your left toes so that almost all your weight is over your left foot. Your right leg should be almost straight and strongly braced so that all your strength is pushing forward.

⑤ Your left hand should slide diagonally up from the right side of your opponent's chest to his left shoulder, palm up, whilst at the same time remaining straight over the line that connects your front and back foot. Thus it is necessary to put into your left arm enough strength as though to cut through your opponent's neck and upper body. Your right hand should be on the same line as your left, at a lower level, as though to chop through your opponent's stomach. Your eyes should look out past the fingertips of your left hand.

Follow the steps above in reverse, making sure to slide your feet, to return your basic stance.

(1)

IMPORTANT POINTS

- Make sure the movement of your left hand is in time with the movement of your left foot.
- Put your weight strongly over your front foot.
- Make sure your shoulders do not rise up with your hands.
- Make sure your body is facing forward, not sideways.
- When you return to the starting position make sure you do not lift your toes.

(2)

(3)

(4)

(5)

TAI NO HENKO 2　体の変更2（押された場合）

Body Movement Exercise Type 2 (When pushed)

This is a basic exercise that trains you to move easily into a safe position and overcome your opponent, by spinning backward on either the left or the right foot, when faced by an opponent who comes at you. There are many kinds and degrees of spin, but this basic movement is, as a first step, performed at 95 degrees.

① Stand facing your opponent in opposite basic stances; you in left and your opponent in right-handed basic stance. Your opponent grasps your left wrist at the back of your hand and pushes. You should not feel as though your left wrist has been taken, but rather that you want your opponent to grasp your wrist. You should spread the fingers of both hands out strongly, maintain a good posture, and feel as though your strength is pushing forward through your fingertips.

② Keeping your weight on your left foot, spin your right foot round behind you 95 degrees, sliding your toes in a large circle. At the same time, without bending your elbow, spin your left hand round in front of you to the right, turning your palm upward, deflecting your opponent's push.

③ Your left hand, palm up, arm almost straight, should be brought round until it is directly over the line of your front knee and level with your opponent's chest. Your right hand, also palm up, should come round at the same level as your stomach, and be parallel with your left arm. Look out past the fingertips of your left hand.

④ Put your weight over your left knee. Your right leg should be almost straight and braced strongly. The distance between your feet should be slightly wider than it was at the beginning of the movement in your basic stance. Make sure your center of gravity is sufficiently lowered and your right hip is pushed strongly forward, so that your upper body cuts across the line of your feet at right angles, giving you a stable posture so that you are able to move again at any time.

Take care to match your opponent's level of intensity, particularly while you are moving, and of course it is important to move smoothly with your opponent's push, neither pulling his hand nor pushing against it.

Finally, follow the steps above in reverse, making sure to slide your feet, to return to your basic stance.

IMPORTANT POINTS

- Make sure not to lift the toes of either foot from the beginning to the end of the exercise.
- Always keep looking forward, not down.
- When placing your weight on your front foot, take care not to bend your back.
- Make sure your arms, legs, and body are all on one line, facing forward, and that your right hip especially does not get left behind.
- While moving, make sure your elbow does not get bent.
- Keep your shoulders down.
- Do not relax when you return to the starting basic stance.
- Take care to perform the exercise slowly and accurately, rather than rushing.
- Make sure your movements, especially those of your arms and legs, are synchronized. Always move in a curve, never in a straight line.

①

②

③

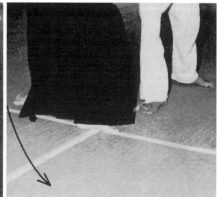

④

HIRIKI NO YOSEI 臂力の養成
Body Line Exercise

The body line exercises are basic movements designed to help you get your arms, legs, and body all on the same line (all moving in unison in the same direction). In performing these exercises, you will also generate strength that comes with timing. You will find that this timing is absolutely essential to the techniques that follow in this book. The power of timing is not just raw power, it is power created through intensity, and combining all the strengths that you have together. The body line exercises are the exercises that enable you to acquire this. While doing this exercise, it is very tempting to lift your toes. Make sure you do not. If your feet leave the floor, your balance and timing will suffer. When sliding your feet forward, make sure your back foot remains at the same angle as it was in your basic stance, pointing outward. When returning to the starting position, a common mistake is to relax. Make sure you keep your level of intensity, so that your body returns to the original stance but remains tensed. Keep looking straight ahead from the beginning to the end of the exercise. When moving backward, move your hands in a downward cutting movement. Do not simply lower your hands. Always keep your weight over your front foot, both when moving forward and backward.

HIRIKI NO YOSEI 1
臂力の養成1 (前進動作)
Body Line Exercise Type 1 (Forward movement)

Many Aikido techniques rely on the same principles as using a sword. Therefore, the basics of using a sword—raising a sword over your head and cutting down—are included in Aikido's basic exercises.

① Stand in the basic stance, right foot forward. Your opponent approaches you from the side and grasps your right wrist with both hands.

② Slide your feet forward, first front foot then back foot, to a distance two thirds of the way between your opponent's feet. Put your weight slightly more over your front foot as you advance. When you move back to your starting stance, slide backward on your back foot first.

①

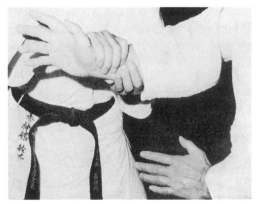

②

③

④

⑤

③ When you move forward, combine all the strength that comes from your legs, lower back, chest, elbows, and wrists into your hands, fingers strongly spread. Pushing forward, raise your hands in a spiral over your forehead as though you are raising a sword.

④⑤ Your right hand should be above your left hand, your elbows slightly to the outside, and your shoulders down. Look straight forward and focus your intensity on pushing strongly forward.

At the beginning of the exercise, your opponent should approach you from the right, and standing left foot forward, should grasp your right wrist at chest height with both hands, without pushing or pulling. Your opponent should not hinder you in the move, so that, even if you are a beginner, it is easier to develop your timing.

When you move forward, your opponent should keep standing left foot forward, but transfer his weight onto his right foot.

IMPORTANT POINTS

- While doing this exercise, it is very tempting to lift your toes. Make sure you do not. If your feet leave the floor, your balance and timing will suffer.

- When sliding your feet forward, make sure your back foot remains at the same angle as it was in your basic stance, pointing outward. When returning to the starting position, a common mistake is to relax. Make sure you keep your level of intensity, so that your body returns to the original stance but remains tensed.

- Keep looking straight ahead from the beginning to the end of the exercise.

- When moving backward, move your hands in a downward cutting movement. Do not simply lower your hands.

- Always keep your weight over your front foot, both when moving forward and backward.

HIRIKI NO YOSEI 2　臂力の養成2（重心の移動）

Body Line Exercise Type 2 (Moving your center of gravity)

When shifting your center of gravity (and moving generally) it is easy to lose your balance. This is a basic exercise that will help you to avoid losing your balance and to move with stability. It will especially help create a stronger and more flexible lower back and legs. It will also help you to develop your ability to derive strength from timing, as in Body Line Exercise Type 1.

① Face your opponent in the basic stance, right foot forward. Have your opponent grasp your right wrist, as in Body Line Exercise Type 1. Turn your upper body anti-clockwise to face the opposite direction, and slide your left foot forward one step. Hold your left hand out at chest height. Your right hand should be placed by your right hip.

② Make sure the fingers of both hands are spread out strongly. Slightly relax your elbows, and keep your shoulders down. You should feel as though power is flowing down through the fingertips on your right hand. Your left knee should be bent strongly and your weight firmly forward. Push down hard with your right foot, without bracing the leg too strongly. Push down with the big toes of both feet, and push your right hip well forward. Stretch your upper body so that the top of your head to the toes of your right foot make a straight line.

③ Shift your weight from your left foot, through your knees, to your right foot. To do this, pivot on the balls of both feet and, turning your body clockwise, drop your right hand down before raising it above your head, pushing though your opponent's thumbs. Your center of gravity should be slightly lower than it was in Body Line Exercise Type 1.

IMPORTANT POINTS

- Note that it is difficult to shift your weight correctly from your right to your left foot.
- Your right hand should only be used to generate power when extending. Make sure you do not pull your opponent with your right hand.
- Strive to be able to shift your weight with both knees bent. Thus there should be no up-down movement of the upper body.
- Always pivot on the balls of your feet, but take care not to lift your heels.
- In the starting position, make sure your right hip is pushed forward strongly. When your hands are raised, make sure your left hip is pushed forward strongly.

①

② ③

SHUMATSU DOSA 終末動作
Finishing Exercises

The Finishing Exercises are directly related to the Multi-Directional throws which are explained at the beginning of Basic Throws. These exercises will help you to improve stability, to move your center of gravity, to raise and cut down with your hands, to manage the distance between you and your opponent, and to get a better feeling of what your opponent is doing. In Aikido the most important thing is to be synchronized with your opponent, and these exercises are very important in learning how your opponent moves. Furthermore, these exercises are useful for your opponent too; as he stretches backward it will help improve his flexibility and back strength and at the same time it is a good workout for his legs and waist.

SHUMATSU DOSA 1　終末動作 1（引かれた場合）
Finishing Exercise Type 1 (When being pulled)

① Stand facing your opponent in the basic Aikido stance. Both you and your opponent stand right foot forward. Your opponent grasps both your wrists and pulls.

② Slide diagonally forward with your right foot, keeping both your hands open, and thrust both hands out in front of you at chest level. Lower your center of balance to get more stability, keep your body vertical, and look straight ahead, past your hands.

③ Your opponent remains right foot forward and his weight shifts to his left foot.

④ Slide your left foot straight forward, well past your opponent. Planting your weight firmly on your left foot, raise your hands up over your head. Your opponent should still be holding both your wrists.

⑤ Pivot on the balls of both feet so that you turn around (to the right) 180 degrees to face the opposite direction. Raise your hands even higher above your head. Bring your left foot up behind your right foot taking care not to raise your heel. Your opponent should ensure that his head is between his arms, which are stretched up and behind him.

⑥ Slide forward with your right foot, and, while extending your arms, cut down with both hands until they are at shoulder level. Put your weight on your front foot and keep your balance.

Your opponent should, pivoting on his right foot, turn his left foot back 180 degrees. He should ensure that your hands are behind his neck without leaning against them. Taking into account the amount your hands are stretched out, if he puts his weight slightly more over his left foot, it will make the exercise somewhat easier.

IMPORTANT POINTS

- Do not let your upper body get bent during point ④.
- It is easy to make the mistake of putting your weight on the wrong foot.
- Do not push against your opponent.
- It is easy to lose your balance if you and your opponent are not moving together.
- Do not let your hands drift from in front of you to one side.
- Do not look down.

Gozo Shioda, dropping to one knee to perform a Timing Throw. (Bringing the opponent instantly off balance and throwing him.)

① ②

③ ④ ⑤

⑥

SHUMATSU DOSA 2　終末動作2（押された場合）

Finishing Exercise Type 2 (When being pushed)

Whereas in Finishing Exercise Type 1 you push forward, in Finishing Exercise Type 2 you spin round to the rear, mastering how to get separation from your opponent, how to raise and cut down with your hands, how to manage the distance between you and your opponent, and get a better understanding of how your opponent is moving.

① Stand facing your opponent in the basic Aikido stance. Your opponent stands right foot forward, you stand left foot forward. Your opponent grasps both your wrists and pushes.

② Keeping your weight on your left foot, slide your right foot around behind you 180 degrees in a big circle so that you end up with your upper body facing in the opposite direction from which you started.

③ Raise your right hand up in front of your face, keeping your elbow down, so that your hand is on the inside of your partner's left wrist. Turn the palm of your left hand up and, using the strength of your opponent who is pushing, swing your hand around in front of you.

④ Turn your upper body around another 180 degrees, and raise both your hands high above your head. Your opponent is still holding your wrists. As a rule, when you turn around do not raise your heels, and slide your back foot (now your left foot) up a little closer to your right foot.

⑤⑥ Slide forward with your right foot. Your back foot should then follow, making sure not to raise your heel. While extending your arms out in front of you, cut down with your hands until they are level with your shoulders.

Your opponent should move sideways, left foot first. He should assume the same posture as in Finishing Exercise Type 1.

IMPORTANT POINTS

- Take care not to bend at the waist. Keep your back straight.
- Move your hands in synchronization.
- Spin your toes in a big, sweeping circular movement.
- When spinning, pivot on the toes of your left foot, and slide the toes of your right foot.
- Pay special attention to the movement of your right hand.
- Always keep your fingers spread open strongly.
- Move in synchronization with your opponent.

①

②

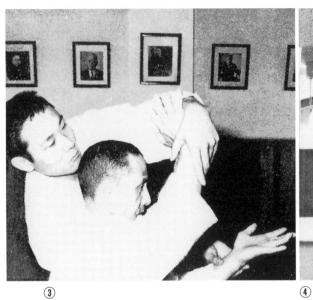

③

④

⑤

⑥

SUWARI WAZA

Throws that start from the kneeling position

The origin of kneeling techniques

Throws from the kneeling position come from the days when part of being a samurai was to be prepared for an enemy at any time and in any circumstance. Such circumstances included, for example, being attacked when asleep, or when attending a lord at his palace. Here the golden rule was never to stand, and to walk on one's knees (so as to ensure you stayed lower than the lord himself). Kneeling techniques were therefore practiced in the same way as standing techniques for self protection in times like these.

The reason for practicing kneeling techniques

It may seem at first glance that practicing kneeling techniques is unnatural in this day and age. So why do it?

If you practice the same throw from both the kneeling and standing stance, you will undoubtedly feel that it is more difficult from the kneeling position. Practicing throws from the kneeling position will strengthen and stabilize your lower back and stomach and enable you to use this strength in all your moves. Thus, the more you train yourself in the kneeling techniques, the easier it will become to perform throws whilst standing.

CHAPTER 2

BASIC TECHNIQUES

基本技法

SHIHO-NAGE　四方投げ
Multi-Directional Throw

In the Multi-Directional Throw, you move as though you are wielding a sword and end up throwing your opponent in the direction of your choice.

In all Aikido throws you must be able to gain control of your opponent right from the start. However, this ability only comes after mastering the Basic Movements, learning the Basic Throws, and lots of practice. The first Basic Throw to explain is the Multi-Directional Throw, in which all the basic elements of Aikido techniques are to be found.

This type of technique includes throws that begin when your opponent grasps one or both wrists or aims a blow to your head, from the front or the side. It can also be used when you start in a kneeling position, and your opponent is standing. In practical application of the technique, the throw may be used in situations where you are grasped and struck at the same time, or even to lock out the arm that grasps you.

Here in Basic Techniques, seven variations of the Multi-Directional Throw are outlined.

KATATE-MOCHI SHIHO-NAGE 1　片手持ち四方投げ 1
Wrist Grasp; Multi-Directional Throw Type 1

In this throw, your opponent can be thrown in any direction after he grasps your left (right) wrist with his right (left) hand and pulls. You start in a similar way to Finishing Exercise Type 1, and finish by locking out your opponent's arm and throwing him onto his back.

① Both you and your opponent stand opposite each other in the basic Aikido stance, right foot forward. When your opponent grasps your left wrist aim a backhanded punch to his face with your right hand. The intention here is to get your opponent to block your punch with his left hand, rather than to actually hit him. That is to say, you force your opponent to protect himself from your punch.

②③④ Sliding your right foot diagonally forward to your right, thrust out your left hand and grasp your opponent's right wrist with your right hand. The fleshy part just below the thumb of your right hand should make contact with your opponent's wrist before you grip it. Your left hand should arc upward as though you are cutting your opponent's stomach with your little finger until your hand is level with your chest. Make sure the palm of your opponent's hand is stuck tightly to your left wrist.

⑤ Take a large sliding step past your opponent with your left foot, putting your weight on your left foot. Raise both your hands up above your eye level.

⑥ Keeping your feet where they are, turn 180 degrees away from your opponent. Transfer your weight from your left foot to your right foot. Extend your right hand and bend your opponent's arm backward over his shoulder as far as it will go.

⑦ Your opponent's wrist should also be bent backward. Slide forward one step with your right foot and drop your opponent onto his back.

⑧ Your right foot should be close alongside your opponent's shoulder. Your left knee should come down near to your right foot. Keeping your opponent's wrist firmly bent, chop down at his face with your left hand. In locking out your opponent's wrist, bend it down and pull it toward you. The throwing of your opponent is really the end of the move, but to practice "locking" the wrist joint, the wrist should be bent firmly until the final blow.

IMPORTANT POINTS

- Give a strong backhand punch.
- Pay close attention to the way you thrust out your left hand.
- Pay close attention to the way you grip with your right hand.
- In point ②, extend your arms.
- In point ③, slide forward with your front foot.
- Always look your opponent in the face and keep a good posture.

①

②

③

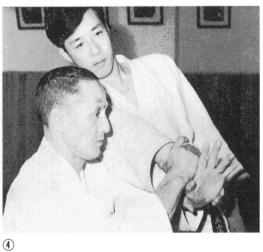

④

⑤

⑥

⑦

⑧

KATATE-MOCHI SHIHO-NAGE 2 片手持ち四方投げ2
Wrist Grasp; Multi-Directional Throw Type 2

In this throw, you use your opponent's strength as he grasps and pushes your wrist by turning your body, locking out your opponent's arm, and throwing him on his back.

① Stand facing your opponent in opposite stances; you left foot forward, your opponent right foot forward. When your opponent grasps your left wrist from the outside with his right hand and pushes, aim a backhanded punch to his face with your right hand.

② Using your opponent's push, pivot on your left foot and spin your right foot around behind you 180 degrees. Keep your weight over your left foot and lower your center of gravity for stability. Bring your left hand (your wrist still being held by your opponent) around and up in a curve to a point past the imaginary line going through your opponent's feet, bending your opponent's wrist out and stretching his arm so that he is off balance. With your right hand, hold your opponent's wrist by first placing your thumb over his pulse and then gripping firmly with your little finger. Hold your opponent's wrist in front of you at your shoulder height.

③ Seen from the opposite direction: transfer a little of your

weight from your left to your right foot and bring both your hands up, so that your opponent appears to hang from his right shoulder.

④ Shift your weight firmly onto your right foot and at the same time turn your upper body clockwise 180 degrees. Bend your opponent's right wrist strongly over his shoulder so that he is unbalanced and nearly falling backward. Slide forward one step and drop your opponent on his back.

⑤ Keep your opponent's wrist bent, and chop down at his face with your left hand.

IMPORTANT POINTS

- Grasp your opponent's wrist while you are spinning your right leg behind you.
- Make sure you extend your opponent's right elbow, so that he "floats."
- In point ③, extend your arms.
- In point ⑤, slide your feet forward.

①

②

③

④

⑤

YOKOMEN UCHI SHIHO-NAGE 1　横面打ち四方投げ1
Strike to the Side of the Head; Multi-Directional Throw Type 1

In this throw, your opponent aims a blow at the side of your head. Without blocking this blow, let your opponent's momentum unbalance him, and throw him onto his back.

①② Stand facing your opponent in the basic stance, both of you right foot forward. When your opponent strikes at the side of your head, slide your right foot half a step diagonally forward and slide your left foot out behind you to the right. With your left hand, cut down the blow that is aimed at your head, and at the same time aim a backhanded punch to your opponent's face.

③ With your left hand, grasp your opponent's right hand just below his thumb, and with your right hand hold your opponent's wrist by first placing your thumb over his pulse. Next, slide forward half a step with your right foot and, twisting your hips to the front, thrust out your hands. Put your weight on your right foot, and hold your arms out at chest level in front of your body. It is very important to push forward, steering with your left hand, and use your right hand to twist your opponent's arm, locking it out.

④ A close-up of ③.

⑤ Make a large sliding step forward, putting your weight onto your left foot, raising your hands above your head.

⑥ Turn your upper body around, and straighten your arms.

⑦ Drop your opponent on his back, keep his wrist bent, and chop down.

IMPORTANT POINTS

- When cutting down with your left hand, spin your left foot in a big circle.
- Your left foot and hand should move at the same time.
- Make sure your opponent is completely off balance.
- Pay special attention to the position of your hands in point ③.
- Pay attention to how you thrust out your hands.
- Always slide your feet.
- Always keep your arms extended.

①

②

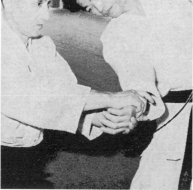

③ ④ ⑤

⑥ ⑦

YOKOMEN UCHI SHIHO-NAGE 2 横面打ち四方投げ2
Strike to the Side of the Head; Multi-Directional Throw Type 2

In this throw, as your opponent starts to aim a strike at the side of your head, you step forward quickly and cut his arm down, lock it out, and throw him on his back.

①② Stand facing your opponent in opposite stances; you left foot forward, your opponent right foot forward. The instant that your opponent aims a blow to the side of your head with his right hand, slide diagonally forward one step with your left foot, and with your left hand chop down on your opponent's right hand. At the same time, aim a backhanded punch to your opponent's face with your right hand.

③ With your left hand, grasp your opponent's right hand just below his thumb. With your right hand take hold of your opponent's wrist by first placing your thumb over his pulse, and at the same time, pivot on your left foot, swinging your right leg round behind you in a large circle.

④ Shift your weight from your left foot to your right foot, turning your upper body clockwise 180 degrees. Stretch out

with your right arm, bending your opponent's arm to its full extent.

⑤ Drop your opponent on his back keeping his wrist bent, and chop down at his face.

IMPORTANT POINTS

- Make your move just as your opponent starts to swing.
- The chop with your left hand, punch with your right hand, and step forward with your left foot should all be simultaneous.
- Do not bend your arms.
- Slide your feet.
- Keep your center of balance low as you spin.

①

②

③

④

⑤

SHOMEN UCHI SHIHO-NAGE   正面打ち四方投げ
Strike to the Forehead; Multi-Directional Throw

① Stand facing your opponent in the basic stance, both of you right foot forward.

②③ Let your opponent's strike to your head meet your right hand at your wrist below your little finger. Pivot on your right foot, sweeping your left foot around behind you, and letting your opponent's momentum carry him forward.

④⑤ Trap your opponent's wrist just below his thumb between the forefinger and thumb of your left hand, and aim a backhanded punch to his face with your right hand. Sliding diagonally forward on your right foot, take hold of your opponent's wrist with your right hand by first placing your thumb over his pulse.

⑥ Take a large sliding step forward with your left foot and, holding your opponent's wrist, raise your hands in front of your forehead.

⑦ Change the direction you are facing, as in Body Line Exercise Type 2, and bend your opponent's arm over his shoulder as though you are cutting down with a sword.

⑧ Sliding forward on your right foot, lower yourself onto your left knee, and drop your opponent.

⑨⑩ Keeping your opponent's wrist still firmly bent, finish the move by chopping down at your opponent's face with your left hand.

①

②

③

④

HANMI HANDACHI KATATE-MOCHI SHIHO-NAGE 1
半身半立ち片手持ち四方投げ 1

Kneeling vs. Standing, Wrist Grasp; Multi-Directional Throw Type 1

This throw starts with you kneeling opposite your opponent. Your opponent grasps your left wrist from the side and pulls. Without standing, you lock his wrist and throw him on his back.

① Assume the kneeling position opposite your opponent. Your opponent stands in the basic stance, right foot forward. He approaches you from the side and with his right hand grasps your left wrist (your hand should be placed on your left knee) and pulls.

② With your left knee, slide forward to a point one third of the way between your opponent's feet. At the same time bend your feet up under you so that you are up on your toes, and your body is firmly sitting over your heels. Thrust out your left hand and with your right hand grasp your opponent's wrist. Your head should be directly under your opponent's armpit, and you should be in a position to look through the gap between your opponent's body and his arm.

③ Raise your left hand in front of your forehead, and transfer your weight from your left to your right knee, putting your opponent off balance so that he is falling backward to his right.

④ Spin round clockwise, stretching out with your right hand to further imbalance your opponent. Your right hand should be at your shoulder height. When turning, if you push your left knee slightly forward, you will be able to keep lower, and lock out your opponent's arm more easily.

⑤ Bend your opponent's wrist and throw him on his back, by sliding forward on your right knee, keeping close to your opponent. Keeping his wrist bent, chop down at his face.

IMPORTANT POINTS

- Move on your knees so that you are up on your toes, which are bent under you.
- Stretch your opponent's right elbow out straight so that his body is lifted up.
- Shift your balance from your left knee to your right knee when you raise your hands.
- When you turn, make sure to keep your arms extended.
- Do not lift your knees up when you move.
- Keep your bottom on your heels.

①

②

③

④

⑤

HANMI HANDACHI RYOTE-MOCHI SHIHO-NAGE 半身半立ち両手持ち四方投げ

Kneeling vs. Standing, Double Wrist Grasp; Multi-Directional Throw

In this throw, you kneel and your opponent stands. When your opponent approaches you from the front and grasps both your wrists, you stand up, spin round, and throw him on his back.

①② Assume the kneeling position opposite your opponent. Your opponent stands in the basic stance, right foot forward. He approaches you and grasps both your wrists (your hands are placed on your knees) and pulls.

③ Slide your left foot forward one step, to a point one third of the way between your opponent's feet. Slide your right knee alongside your left heel, and come up on the toes of your right foot. Thrust out your left hand, and with your right hand grasp hold of your opponent's right wrist.

④⑤ Raising your hands up in front of your forehead, stand up. Spin round clockwise, swinging your right leg around behind you. This is so that when you bend your opponent's wrist back over his shoulder, you are in a good position to bring him off balance.

⑧ Slide forward one step with your back (right) foot, dropping your opponent on his back. Keeping his wrist bent, chop down at his face.

IMPORTANT POINTS

- Slide forward with your left foot before you stand.
- Swing your right leg around behind you and spin around at the same time as you raise your hands.
- Keep your arms straight.
- When you step forward with your right foot, remember to slide your foot.
- Keep your hips down.
- Let your opponent grasp your wrists by placing your hands on your knees.

① ② ③

④

⑤

⑥

IKKAJO-OSAE 一ヵ条抑え
First Control

First Control is the name given to the technique where you focus your attack on your opponent's elbow joint to get him off balance and under your control.
A variation of the technique is the "First Control Throw," but these throws will be explained in a later section.

The moves involved in First Control are based on the principles of techniques such as raising and cutting down with a sword, thrusting with a spear, and using your whole body to push your opponent. You will learn the correct spacing between you and your opponent when he is diagonally in front of you, how to move forward at an angle, how to use the strength in your lower back, and how to use your opponent's momentum. When practicing the moves as the opponent, you will also be able to train and strengthen your elbows. Thus, First Control is a very important basic technique

SUWARI WAZA SHOMEN UCHI IKKAJO-OSAE 1
座り技正面打ち一ヵ条抑え 1
Kneeling Strike to the Forehead; First Control Type 1

① Both you and your opponent kneel, facing each other. The distance between your knees and the knees of your opponent should be roughly equivalent to two fists. The space between your own knees should be about one fist. Keep your back straight and your shoulders down. Both hands should be placed loosely on your lap. Look your opponent squarely in the eyes.

② You make a preemptive strike against your opponent by raising your hands and chopping straight forward with your right hand at his forehead. Your opponent blocks this attack with his right wrist. With your left hand, grasp your opponent's right elbow from below, thrusting upward.

When chopping and blocking this attack, your right arm and the right arm of your opponent should not be completely straight. It is especially important to bend your opponent's elbow when you make contact with his right wrist. A slightly bent elbow allows you to push harder than with a straight arm, and protects your elbow joint at the same time.

③ ② seen from the reverse angle.

④ Slide your right knee forward diagonally to the right, and at the same time cut down in a circular movement with your right hand, whilst thrusting up with your left hand, pushing your opponent's elbow up and to the right, completely unbalancing him.

⑤ Push your hips and waist strongly to the right, and having cut down with your right hand, grasp your opponent's wrist in front of your right hip. Having thrust upward with your left hand, press down hard on your opponent's elbow joint from above, getting him under control.

⑥ Slide your left knee forward in the direction of your opponent's waist. Thrust your opponent's arm, which you are holding, like a spear in the direction of his shoulder. When you move forward diagonally to the right with your right knee, your opponent should now be completely prone.

⑦ Stretch your opponent's arm out from his body 90 degrees, and put your left knee tight beside his ribs under his arm. Place your right knee down by your opponent's right wrist, which you are still holding in your right hand, just by your own thumb. Press down hard with your left hand on his elbow joint, as though you are stretching his arm.

⑧ In the finishing move, do not overly bend your left wrist, but push straight down from above without grasping with your left hand. Let your strength flow in the direction of your wrist, using the natural "L" shape of your arm and hand. This method allows you to stretch your opponent's right arm, locking it out, effectively stopping any resistance.

IMPORTANT POINTS

- As soon as you start the move, make sure you stay up on your toes. In the case of all techniques practiced from the kneeling position, it is true to say that it is easier to move when you are up on your toes. You can use this leverage to enable you to push with your feet, and it gives you more stability. This exercise will train your feet, and as your toes become stronger, you will be able to use this strength to good effect when you practice throws from the standing position.

- When you kneel, maintain a good posture and keep looking your opponent in the eyes.
- In point ②, make sure to strike straight at your opponent's head. Be careful not to fall into the common mistake of aiming your strike at your opponent's hand.
- In point ②, do not grasp your opponent's wrist. Aim to cut his hand down with the side of your hand. Grasp his wrist for the first time in point ④.

- In all moves practiced from the kneeling position, make sure you do not raise your hips.
- When moving your knees, do not raise your knees off the ground. Your heels should also be kept together, the back foot moving with the movement of the front foot.
- Do not over-focus on trying to control your opponent's right arm to such an extent that the spacing between you becomes cramped.

①

②

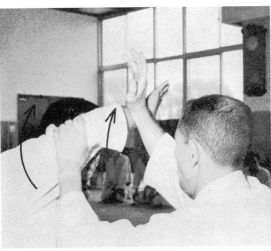

③

④

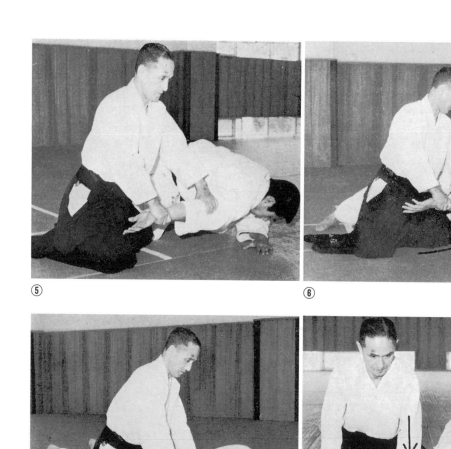

⑤   ⑥

⑦   ⑧

SHOMEN UCHI IKKAJO-OSAE 1 (TACHI WAZA) 正面打ち一ヵ条抑え1（立ち技）
Strike to the Forehead; First Control Type 1 From the standing position

Hereafter the term "from the standing position" will be omitted. If the term "kneeling" is not used in the name, the reader should assume that the move begins from the standing position.

This throw uses the same moves and techniques as the kneeling version previously explained, but from the standing position.

① You and your opponent stand facing each other in the basic stance, right foot forward.

② Raise your right hand and, sliding forward leading with your right foot, chop with the side of your hand at your opponent's forehead. Your opponent blocks this attack with his right wrist. Placing your weight on your front foot, with your left hand, grasp your opponent's right elbow from below, thrusting upward, allowing you to gain the initiative. The movement of both your and your partner's hands is identical to that in the kneeling version of the throw.

③ Slide diagonally forward to the right with your right foot, sliding forward a little with your left foot too. Cut down with your hands in the same way explained in the kneeling technique.

④ Twist your hips to the right, putting your weight on an imaginary line that runs through your right foot and your left hand, pressing down on your opponent's right arm. Your face, upper body, and lower back should all be facing to the right. Your right knee should be bent to keep your body low. In this way you are able to put even more pressure on your opponent.

⑤ After you have got your opponent under control, slide your left foot forward in the direction of his side, or in other words

diagonally to the left, putting your weight on it. At the same time, in the same way as explained in the kneeling version of the throw, keeping his arm under control, thrust it in the direction of his shoulder.

⑥ Slide forward to the right on your right foot. At the same time, stretch out your opponent's arm, applying more pressure on it. Put your left knee down tight against your opponent's side, under his arm.

⑦ Put your right knee and your opponent's wrist down at the same time. Finish the move, applying the elbow lock, in the same way as the kneeling version.

IMPORTANT POINTS

- Take the initiative by striking at your opponent.

- Your left and right hand should make contact with your opponent's right arm simultaneously.

- In point ④, bend your right knee strongly.

- In points ④ and ⑤, it is easy to fall into the mistake of pulling in your opponent's arm. Take care to keep your arms straight, and apply pressure with your whole body.

- From points ② to ⑥, point your toes in the direction you are moving in. Always slide your feet.

- The finishing move, locking your opponent's arm, is carried out in the same way as in the kneeling version. Breathe out as you apply the pressure.

- This move forces your opponent gradually lower and lower. A common mistake is to bend your back. Make sure you keep your back straight and a good posture at all times.

①

②

③

④

⑤

⑥

⑦

SUWARI WAZA SHOMEN UCHI IKKAJO-OSAE 2　座り技正面打ち一ヵ条抑え 2
Kneeling Strike to the Forehead; First Control Type 2

Unlike First Control Type 1, in this throw you use your opponent's momentum as he strikes at you, using the First Control technique to force him into submission.

① You and your opponent kneel facing each other. Look your opponent in the eyes. (This is the same for all Aikido moves.)

② Your opponent raises his right hand and strikes, chopping at your forehead. Block the blow with your right wrist, and catch your opponent's elbow with your left hand.

　The angle of your right forearm should be almost identical to that employed in the First Control Type 1 throw. Your right arm should find this correct angle easily, but as the left arm has a tendency to bend too much at the elbow, stretch your left hand out slightly and grasp the elbow. If your left arm is bent, your opponent's strength will double, and the spacing between you will become tighter, making it extremely difficult to move. Block with the right hand and stretch with the left, so that your hands work to push your opponent's momentum upward.

　Of course, as soon as your opponent starts to move, get up on your toes, and keep your hips down.

③④⑤ Cut down in a circular motion with your right hand. With your left hand, thrust your opponent's elbow up and over before cutting down. Putting your weight on your left knee, spin your right knee around behind you 270 degrees, turning your opponent's right arm around in the same direction, cutting downward at the same time.

　Of course, you must keep both your arms straight, keeping the same spacing between you and your opponent as you move.

⑥ Fix your opponent's arm to the floor, and apply the final lock in exactly the same way as in First Control Type 1.

IMPORTANT POINTS

- In point ②, though your opponent strikes first, it is important that you feel that you are one step ahead of your opponent, ready for his move.

- In point ③, it is important that your left hand and right wrist make contact with your opponent's arm at the same time. Also, at the same time, you should get up onto your toes and keep your hips down pushing your whole body weight forward to block your opponent's strike. It is vitally important not to be driven back.

- When spinning around to the rear, take care that your knees and toes do not float up off the floor.

- Keep looking forward as you spin. Take care not to bend your upper body, especially your back.

- Do not grab with your right hand, use your wrist to lead. Only once your opponent's momentum has carried him around, grasp his wrist.

- Make sure your arms and legs move at the same time. Take special care that you do not spin round with your legs first then pull your opponent with your arms.

- From the start to the finish of the throw make sure you do not bend your arms or raise your shoulders.

①

②

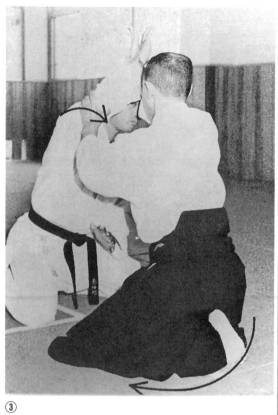

③

④

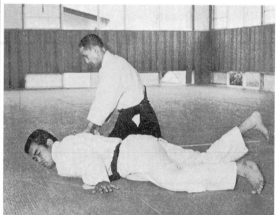

⑤

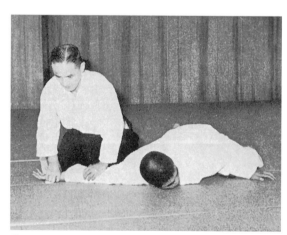

⑥

SHOMEN UCHI IKKAJO-OSAE 2 正面打ち一ヵ条抑え 2
Strike to the Forehead; First Control Type 2

① Stand left foot forward, facing your opponent who is standing right foot forward. Block your opponent's strike to your forehead with your right wrist, and with your left hand make contact with his elbow.

②③④ Pivot on your left foot, spinning your right foot around behind you 180 degrees, allowing your opponent to be carried forward by his momentum. Transfer your weight from your left foot to your right foot, and turn your upper body to face the opposite direction, whilst at the same time lowering yourself down onto your left knee, causing your opponent to be thrown flat onto his face.

⑤⑥ Put your right knee down. Stretch your opponent's right arm out, and with your left hand push down hard on his elbow joint, locking it out.

①

②

③

④

⑤

⑥

YOKOMEN UCHI IKKAJO-OSAE 1 　横面打ち一ヵ条抑え 1
Strike to the Side of the Head; First Control Type 1

You and your opponent stand facing each other in the basic stance, right foot forward. Your opponent strikes at the left side of your head with the side of his right hand.

①② Slide half a step forward diagonally to the left with both feet, turning slightly to your left at the same time. Block your opponent's strike with your left wrist, and at the same time aim a backhanded punch at his face with your right hand.

③ Place your right wrist over your left forearm, making a cross and trapping your opponent's right wrist.

④ Sliding diagonally forward to the right with your right foot, with your right hand cut down your opponent's right hand, and at the same time thrust his elbow upward from below with your left hand.

⑤ Turn your hips strongly to the right and put your weight firmly over your right foot. Push down on your opponent's arm with both hands, forcing him to the ground.

　Here, in the same way as in the Strike to the Forehead First Control types 1 and 2 techniques, straighten your left arm and lower your left shoulder, applying strong pressure on your opponent's right arm.

⑥ Slide diagonally forward to the left with your left foot, thrusting your opponent's arm in the direction of his shoulder.

⑦⑧ Bring your right foot up level with your left foot, kneel, and apply the finishing arm lock.

①

②

③

④

⑤

⑥

⑦

⑧

SUWARI WAZA YOKOMEN UCHI IKKAJO-OSAE 2 　座り技横面打ち一ヵ条抑え 2
Kneeling Strike to the Side of the Head; First Control Type 2

①②③ You and your opponent kneel opposite each other. Your opponent strikes at the left side of your head with the side of his right hand. As soon as your opponent starts to move, slide to your left on your knees and, blocking the strike with your left wrist, aim a backhanded punch to his face with your right hand.

④ Point 3, seen from the reverse angle.

⑤ In the same way as in the Strike to the Side of the Head; First Control Type 1 technique, cross your right hand over your left, and trap your opponent's wrist between your wrists.

⑥ With your weight placed over your left knee, pivot on it, spinning your right knee around behind you in the same way as in the Strike to the Forehead; First Control Type 2 technique. Slide your left hand down to your opponent's elbow and grasp it. Thrusting up with your left hand, and cutting down with your right, push your opponent off balance.

Shift your weight further in the same direction as your spin, cutting down your opponent's wrist in the same direction.

⑦ Place your opponent's arm on the floor, and apply the First Control arm lock.

As this throw is almost the same as the Kneeling Strike to the Forehead Type 2 throw, it may appear easy. However, when you actually practice it, you will find it an unexpectedly difficult technique that will require a lot of practice to master.

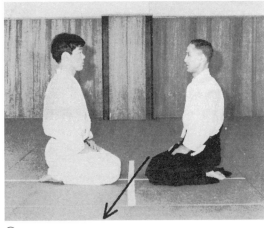

①

②

③

④

⑤

⑥

⑦

YOKOMEN UCHI IKKAJO-OSAE 2　横面打ち一ヵ条抑え 2

Strike to the Side of the Head; First Control Type 2

Stand facing your opponent left foot forward. Your opponent, standing right foot forward, strikes at the left side of your head with the side of his right hand.

① Slide diagonally forward to the left, leading with your left foot.

② Get the jump on your opponent by immediately flying in, blocking the strike with your left wrist. In this case it is important to push your wrist to the outside, deflecting your opponent's momentum. Of course, stiffen your underarm and keep your shoulder down as you do this. Also ensure that your weight is firmly on your front foot, and that your right foot is not left behind. At the same time, aim a backhanded punch to your opponent's face with your right hand.

③ In the same way as in the kneeling technique, trap your opponent's wrist between your crossed hands.

④ Spin your right foot around behind you 180 degrees, cutting down with your right hand. As your opponent's elbow makes contact with your left hand, thrust it upward bringing him off balance.

⑤ Transfer your weight back onto your right foot, turning your hips around to the right. Guide your opponent round while applying pressure to his right elbow, and set your left knee down on the floor.

⑥ Put your right knee down as you put your opponent's arm down flat on the floor, and apply the First Control arm lock.

①

②

③

④

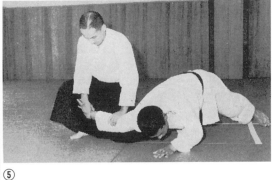

⑤

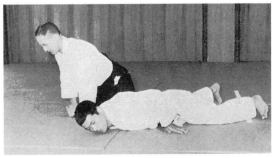

⑥

Up to this point, we have only looked at throws that start when your opponent grasps your wrist or strikes at your head with the side of his hand. Now, we move onto throws using the First Control that start when your opponent grasps your shirt in front of your shoulder.

In Aikido there are exercises that are designed to train individual body areas, and others to develop co-ordination. This throw will also help you to focus all your bodily strength in your shoulder.

①② Both you and your opponent kneel opposite each other. Your opponent grasps your shirt in front of your left shoulder with his right hand and pulls. Your opponent should grasp your shirt so that the back of his fist is facing upward, and he should make sure his thumb is not sticking out.

From the instant your shirt is grasped, it is important to make all movements, consciously focusing on your shoulder.

③ With the idea of shifting the direction of your opponent's pull, slide your left knee to the left. Pull your left hand out in the same direction, and with the back of your right hand, aim a punch at your opponent's face. Of course, as soon as you start to move, get up on your toes.

④⑤ With your right hand, take hold of the back of your opponent's right fist, and keep it pressed tightly against your shoulder. Slide diagonally forward to the right with your right knee, and with your left wrist, thrust your opponent's right elbow upward from below, forcing him off balance. (Your left wrist and your left shoulder should push forward.)

⑥ Turn your hips to the right, and shift your weight on your right side. Cut down strongly with your left hand.

⑦ Taking hold of your opponent's elbow with your left hand, slide your left knee diagonally forward in the direction of your opponent's side, thrusting his right arm in the direction of his shoulder. Take care at this point to keep your opponent's hand fixed to your shoulder, maintaining a posture so that your upper body is pushing down on your opponent's hand.

⑧ Slide forward on your right knee, and keeping your opponent's elbow straight and wrist firmly bent, put his arm down flat on the floor, at a 90-degree angle to his body. Apply more pressure to both his wrist and elbow, locking his arm to the floor.

⑨ Your left knee should be placed tight against your opponent's side under his arm, and your right knee should be right next to his bent wrist. In the same way as the Strikes to the Forehead and Side of the Head; First Control techniques, press down on his elbow with your left hand. Lay your opponent's wrist flat on the floor, and bend his hand back strongly in the direction of his shoulder.

IMPORTANT POINTS

- Thrust your opponent's elbow upward in the direction of his right ear. Cut down strongly.

- Up to point ⑦, do not remove your opponent's hand from your shoulder.

- In point ⑧, do not try to lock your opponent's arm with your hands alone. Use your whole body to push.

①

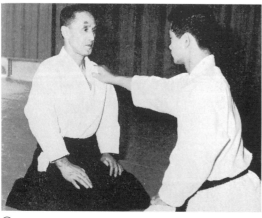

②

③

(4)

(5)

(6)

(7)

(8)

(9)

This throw is the same as the kneeling version, conducted from the standing position.

① Both you and your opponent stand facing each other, right foot forward. Your opponent grasps your shirt at the front of your left shoulder and pulls.

②③④⑤ Aim a backhanded punch with your right hand at your opponent's face. Slide to your left, leading with your left foot, and following with your right. Concentrate your strength into your left shoulder. With your right hand, in the same way as in the kneeling technique, grasp the back of your opponent's right fist from above, and keep it pressed tightly against your shoulder. Slide diagonally forward to the right with your right foot, and with your left wrist thrust his right elbow upward.

⑥ Turn your hips strongly to the right, and shift your weight even more firmly onto your right foot. With your left hand, cut down on your opponent's right arm, forcing him to the floor.

⑦ Change the position of your left hand that is pressing down on your opponent's elbow to grasp the elbow, and slide your left foot forward diagonally to the left, into his side. Push his arm strongly in the direction of his shoulder, forcing him even lower to the floor.

⑧ Slide diagonally forward to the right on your right foot, putting your weight on your right foot. Fix your opponent's right arm to the floor, keeping his elbow locked and wrist bent.

⑨ Apply the final push.

IMPORTANT POINTS

- In point ②, you must move with your weight remaining over your right foot. This is necessary to allow you to move quickly and strongly to your right in the next move.

- In point ⑥, it is easy to allow your back to become bent. Take care to lower your stance, and not to bend your back. This is important as it allows you to put all your weight onto one straight line.

- Until point ⑦, do not remove your opponent's right hand from your shoulder.

①

②

③

④

⑤

⑥

⑦

⑧

⑨

SUWARI WAZA KATA-MOCHI IKKAJO-OSAE 2　座り技肩持ち一ヵ条抑え 2

Kneeling Shoulder Grasp; First Control Type 2

In this throw, when your opponent grasps your shirt in front of your shoulder and pushes, you use the First Control to force him into submission.

①②③ You and your opponent kneel opposite each other. With his right hand, your opponent grasps your shirt in front of your shoulder (using the same grip as for the type 1 technique) and pushes. Slide your left knee to the left, get up on your toes, and aim a backhanded punch to your opponent's face with your right hand.

④ With your right hand, grasp the back of your opponent's fist and fix it to your shoulder. Pull your right knee back behind you and, thrusting your left shoulder out, with your left wrist push his right elbow upward.

⑤⑥⑦ Spin your right knee around behind you in a large circle. As your body turns to the right, with your left hand cut down strongly in the same direction on your opponent's elbow.

⑧ As per Type 1 of the same technique, apply the finishing First Control elbow and wrist lock.

IMPORTANT POINTS

- In point ③, place your weight slightly more over your left knee than your right.

- In point ④, your left hand must be in line with your knees, lower back, and face. Your center of balance should be firmly over your left knee.

- In points ⑤, ⑥, and ⑦, when spinning make sure your right knee remains in contact with the floor at all times. Also ensure that your left arm remains stretched out, and that you cut down in a wide circular movement. As per the Strikes to the Forehead and Side of the Head; First Control techniques, you should always keep your head facing forward through your turn.

①

②

③

④

Gozo Shioda, performing a Timing Throw as his opponent rushes in.
(The opponent is thrown using split second timing.)

⑤

⑥

⑦

⑧

KATA-MOCHI IKKAJO-OSAE 2　肩持ち一ヵ条抑え 2

Shoulder Grasp; First Control Type 2

This throw is the same as the kneeling version, conducted from the standing position.

①②③ Stand facing your opponent left foot forward. When your opponent, standing right foot forward, grasps your shirt in front of your shoulder and pushes, slide diagonally forward to the left. Lead with your left foot, and follow with your right. Aim a backhanded punch to your opponent's face with your right hand. Keep your weight on your left foot.

④ With your right hand, grasp the back of your opponent's fist and fix it to your shoulder. Slide your right foot back behind you about 45 degrees, and at the same time with your left wrist push your opponent's elbow upward so that he is lifted up and off balance.

⑤⑥ Spin your right foot around clockwise behind you in a wide circle 180 degrees, and at the same time with your left hand cut down strongly in the same direction on your opponent's elbow, forcing him down.

⑦ Transfer your weight onto your right foot and kneel on your left knee, forcing your opponent flat onto the floor.

⑧ Finally, kneel with your right knee as you place your opponent's wrist on the floor, and apply the finishing arm lock.

IMPORTANT POINTS

- In point ③, unlike the Type 1 version of the First Control, in order to allow you to spin round to the rear, place your weight on your left foot. Your left hand should be in line with both your feet. Make sure you keep your fingers spread open stiffly.

- In point ④, when you thrust your opponent's elbow upward with your left wrist, it is important to push out with your left shoulder, which makes it easier to raise your opponent's right arm. It is also important to thrust your opponent's elbow up as you push your wrist round to the inside.

- In points ⑤ and ⑧, cut down on your opponent's arm with the feeling as though you are chopping him diagonally in two, from one shoulder to his opposite hip

①

②

③

④

⑤

⑥

⑦

⑧

KATATE-MOCHI IKKAJO-OSAE 1 　片手持ち一ヵ条抑え 1
Wrist Grasp; First Control Type 1

①② You and your opponent stand facing each other, right foot forward. Your opponent grasps your left wrist with his right hand and pulls.

③④ Slide to your left, and aim a backhanded punch with your right hand to your opponent's face.

⑤ Thrust your opponent's right hand upward with your left wrist, making sure his thumb is trapped against your wrist, lifting him off balance. With your right hand, grasp the back of his wrist.

⑥ Turn your hips strongly to the right, and cut down with your left hand, keeping your opponent's thumb and wrist locked.

⑦ Slide diagonally forward to the left with your left foot. With your right hand, keep your opponent's wrist bent. With your left hand push down strongly on his elbow joint. Thrust your opponent's arm strongly in the direction of his shoulder, forcing him downward.

⑧ Slide diagonally forward to the right with your right foot, bringing your left knee down to the floor. Finally, kneel with your right knee as you place your opponent's wrist on the floor, and apply the First Control arm lock.

①

②

③

④

⑤

⑥

⑦

⑧

KATATE-MOCHI IKKAJO-OSAE 2　片手持ち一ヵ条抑え2

Wrist Grasp; First Control Type 2

①② Stand left foot forward facing your opponent, who stands right foot forward. Your opponent grasps your left wrist and pushes.

③ Slide to your left and aim a backhanded punch to your opponent's face with your right hand. Slide your right foot round behind you in a circle, and stretch out your opponent's right arm.

④⑤ Spin your right foot round behind you once more, in a wide circle, thrusting up with your left hand. Spin once more in the same direction and, keeping your opponent's wrist and thumb locked, cut down in a curve with your left wrist.

⑥⑦ Transfer your weight onto your right foot, turning your upper body around to the right. Finally fix your opponent's wrist and elbow to the floor and apply the First Control arm lock.

IMPORTANT POINTS

- When your wrist is grasped, take care to keep your fingers spread straight out stiffly.

- In points ③, ④, and ⑤, make all your movements large and circular, not straight.

①

②

③

④

Gozo Shioda, catching his opponent's head between his hands and feet, brings him off balance and throws him.

⑤

⑥

⑦

USHIRO WAZA RYOTE-MOCHI IKKAJO-OSAE 1 後ろ技両手持ち一ヵ条抑え 1

Double Wrist Grasp from Behind; First Control Type 1

① Stand right foot forward. Your opponent comes round behind you and grasps both your wrists and pulls.

②③ Slide your left foot slightly diagonally backward to the left, lowering your body and your center of gravity. Bend your wrists, taking some of the strength out of your opponent's pull.

④ As if you were raising a sword over your head, with your opponent still holding both wrists, bring your hands up over your head, lifting your opponent up and off balance.

⑤ Swing your right foot back to the left in a big curve, bringing your head and body through under your opponent's left hand, pushing him forward and off balance.

⑥ With your right hand grasp your opponent's left elbow, and with your left hand grasp his left wrist at the back of his hand.

⑦ Turn your hips strongly to the right, and cut down strongly, forcing your opponent downward.

⑧ Slide forward with your right foot.

⑨ Apply the First Control arm lock.

IMPORTANT POINTS

- In point ②, bend your wrists and lower your body without bending your elbows.

- In point ④, bring your hands, palms up, in front of you in a big egg-shaped curve.

- In point ⑤, stretch your right foot out behind you, lowering your body, and placing your weight on your left foot.

①

②

③

④

⑤

⑥

⑦

⑧

⑨

USHIRO WAZA RYOTE-MOCHI IKKAJO-OSAE 2 　後ろ技両手持ち一ヵ条抑え2
Double Wrist Grasp from Behind; First Control Type 2

①② Stand right foot forward. Your opponent comes round behind you and grasps both your wrists and pushes. Lower your body and bend your wrists to unbalance your opponent.

③ Bringing both hands up over your head in a curve, sweep your left foot, toes facing to the right, around in front of you, and turn your upper body to face your opponent.

④ Grasp your opponent's left elbow with your right hand, and his left wrist with your left hand.

⑤⑥ In the same manner as in other First Control Type 2 techniques, pivot on your right foot, spinning your left foot around behind you to throw down your opponent.

⑦ Apply the First Control arm lock to finish.

IMPORTANT POINTS

- Always lead and unbalance your opponent by moving in a curve. Never move in a straight line.

①

②

Gozo Shioda, as his opponent goes to grab his right knee with both hands, brings him off balance and throws him.

③

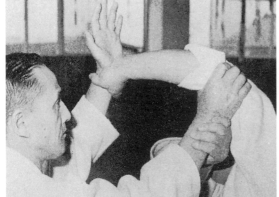

④

⑤

⑥

⑦

NIKAJO-OSAE 二ヵ条抑え
Second Control

Second Control is the name given to the technique where you bend your opponent's arm, causing pain in his wrist joint, in order to unbalance him and force him face down on the floor. In all throws using the Second Control, you apply a finishing arm lock with your opponent face down on the floor.

NIKAJO-SHIME NO KATA 二ヵ条締めの形
The Various Forms of the Second Control Technique

KATATE-MOCHI (TEKUBI-DORI) 片手持ち（手首取り）
From a wrist grasp—where you grasp your opponent's hand and wrist

When your opponent grasps your left wrist with his right hand, use your opponent's weight to move into a position to bring him off balance. Bring your left hand up in a circle, trapping your opponent's wrist between your thumb and forefinger. With the palm of your right hand, cover and hold the back of your opponent's right hand. Gripping tightly with the little fingers of both hands, put your whole body weight into your hands, cutting downward as though with a sword, and locking your opponent's wrist joint.

①

②

③

KATATE-MOCHI (TEGATANA-SHIME) 片手持ち（手刀締め）

From a wrist grasp—applied with the side of your hand

This is similar to the technique above, but in this case you do not grasp your opponent's wrist. Bring your left hand up in a circle and place the side of your hand over your opponent's wrist. Hold the back of his hand in your right palm, trapping his right arm between your left wrist, which he is holding, and your right hand. Cut down with the side of your hand toward your opponent's armpit, locking his wrist joint.

①

②

③

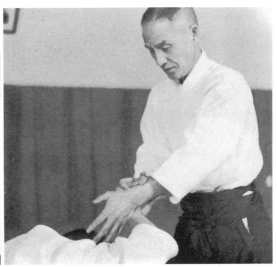

④

HIJI-MOCHI (HIJI-ATE) 肘持ち (肘当)
From an elbow grasp—applied with your elbow

When your opponent grasps your sleeve by your left elbow, lift your opponent's elbow by sliding your own arm upward against it. In a similar fashion to the Second Control from a wrist grasp applied with the side of your hand, this time place your elbow over your opponent's wrist, and cut down, locking his wrist joint. Especially when you place your elbow on your opponent's wrist, be careful not to allow your hips to rise, your body to stretch forward, or your shoulders to become tense. It is important to keep your arms in, your weight on your front foot, and the correct spacing between you and your opponent.

①

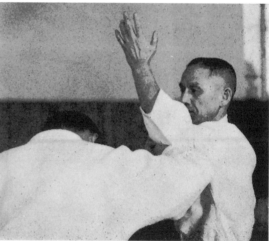

②

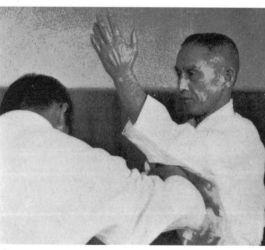

③

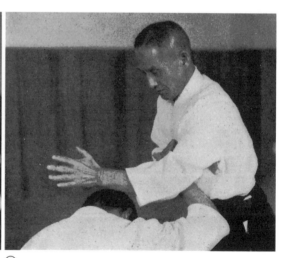

④

KATA-MOCHI (KATA-KOTEI) 肩持ち (肩固定)

From a shoulder grasp—where you fix your opponent's hand to your shoulder

In the case where your opponent grasps your shirt in front of your shoulder, you fix his hand to your shoulder before locking his wrist joint. When your opponent grasps your shirt in front of your left shoulder with his right hand, hold his right hand in your right palm from above, fixing it to your shoulder. At the same time, thrusting your left shoulder forward,

lift your opponent's arm by sliding your left arm upward against it, and continue by bending his arm in toward you. Taking hold of his wrist, without relaxing your grip and keeping your shoulder pushed forward, put your weight into your shoulder and hands, and lock his wrist joint.

①

②

③

④

KATATE AYA-MOCHI (AYA-TEKUBI-DORI) 片手綾持ち（綾手首取り）

From a wrist grasp when your opponent grasps your wrist from above

In the case where your opponent grasps your wrist from above, flip your wrist over the top and apply the wrist lock in the same way as in the Second Control from a wrist grasp applied with the side of the hand. When your opponent grasps your right wrist with his right hand, turn your hand over, moving from the inside to the outside in a curve, placing the side of your right hand on top of your opponent's wrist. With your left hand, cover your opponent's right hand with your palm, so that your opponent's hand is locked between your left hand and your right arm. With the side of your hand, cut down and lock his wrist joint.

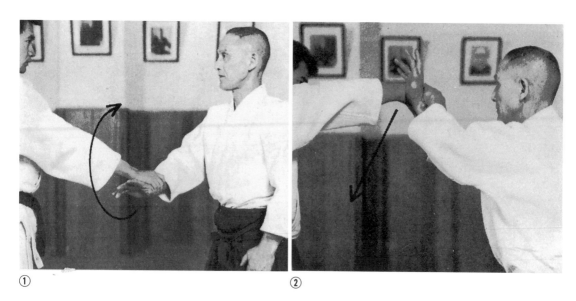

① ②

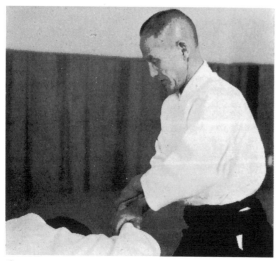

③

SHOMEN-UCHI (TEKUBI-DORI) 正面打ち（手首取り）

From a strike to the forehead where you grasp your opponent's wrist and hand

From a situation like that in the Strike to the Forehead; First Control Type 1 throw, when you have cut down your opponent's arm in front of you, you use the same technique as in the Second Control from a wrist grasp (where you hold your opponent's hand and wrist). As the method of getting hold of your opponent's hand and wrist from this position is very difficult, special care is needed. Starting from the position where you have cut your opponent's arm down in front of

you, slide your left hand, which is holding his elbow, down to his wrist. Relax your grip with your right hand by letting go with your thumb. Slide your thumb around from the outside to the inside of your opponent's wrist so that you scoop up the back of your opponent's hand in the palm of your hand. However, you must do this at the same time as moving your body into position, so care is needed to maintain overall balance.

①

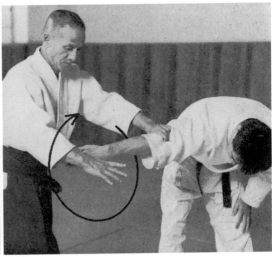

②

③

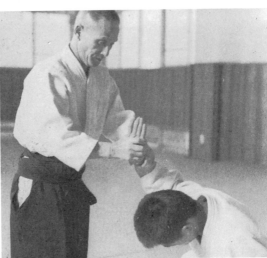

④

NIKAJO NO OSAE-KATA 二ヵ条の抑え方
Application of the Second Control Finishing Arm Lock (Pin)

① This is the position where you have forced your opponent flat onto his stomach.

② Twist to your right so that you are facing your opponent's head and shoulders. At the same time, trap his forearm in the fold of your left elbow.

③ Grasp your own lapel with your left hand.

④ Place the side of your right hand against your opponent's elbow, and fix his arm to your chest.

⑤ Turning at the hips, change the direction of your upper body, locking your opponent's arm.

①

②

③

④

⑤

SUWARI WAZA KATATE-MOCHI NIKAJO-OSAE 1　座り技片手持ち二ヵ条抑え 1

Kneeling Wrist Grasp; Second Control Type 1

① You and your opponent stand facing each other, right foot forward in the basic stance. Both of you step forward and kneel. Your opponent grasps your left wrist with his right hand and pulls.

② Using the strength of your opponent's pull, move diagonally forward to the left, and at the same time aim a backhanded punch with your right hand to his face.

③ Returning to the inside, swing your left hand up and round in a circular movement and grasp your opponent's hand and wrist using the method described in Second Control from a wrist grasp where you grasp your opponent's hand and wrist.

④ Fixing your hips and lower back into a stable position, tense the muscles under your arms, and cut down on your opponent's wrist as though you are cutting down with a sword.

⑤ Without relaxing the Second Control wrist lock, turn your right hand forward, with your left hand grasp your opponent's elbow, and slide forward on your right knee, turning your hips in that direction.

⑥ Leading with your left knee, thrust toward your opponent's underarm. Move your hands, feet, and lower back together.

⑦ In order to force your opponent flat to the floor, slide forward on your right knee.

IMPORTANT POINTS

- The movements involved in this technique are almost identical to those used in the standing version. However, in the kneeling version special care is needed as it is easy for your hips to rise up and your feet to get tangled up.

- Although the finishing Second Control arm lock (pin) is basically the same for all Second Control throws, one slight difference for throws that start from the kneeling position is that both knees are down when you apply it.

- In point ②, when you move sideways, do not just lean with your upper body, but move your whole body to the side.

- In point ⑤, turn your opponent's arm over, turn your hips to the right, and slide forward on your right knee all at the same time. Your upper body should be leaning forward, but do not allow your hips to rise.

①

②

③

④

⑤

⑥

⑦

KATATE-MOCHI NIKAJO-OSAE 1 片手持ち二ヵ条抑え 1

Wrist Grasp; Second Control Type 1

① You and your opponent stand facing each other in the basic stance, right foot forward. Your opponent grasps your left wrist with his right hand and pulls.

② When your opponent pulls your wrist, make a small circular movement to the outside, thrusting your left hand out to the side, and at the same time, aim a backhanded punch with your right hand to your opponent's face.

③ Bring both your hands round and up in front of you in a circular motion, grasping your opponent's hand and wrist. At the same time slide back in a curve, slightly to the inside, with both feet, so as to gain a comfortable spacing with your opponent.

④ Cut down on your opponent's hand along your body's own center line and slightly pushing toward your opponent (as though you are cutting down with a sword).

⑤ Without relaxing your control of your opponent's wrist, turn your opponent's wrist away from you with your right hand, and slide your left hand down from his wrist to his elbow. Grasping his elbow, slide forward on your right foot, turning your hips to the right.

⑥ Slide your left foot in toward your opponent's side, moving your hands, back, and feet at the same time, further unbalancing your opponent.

⑦ Slide forward on your right foot, dropping your opponent flat to the floor, and kneeling with your left knee. Shift your body so that you are facing your opponent, trapping his arm in the fold of your left elbow. Apply the side of your right hand to your opponent's elbow, as though to bend it. Fix your opponent's arm to your chest and, turning your hips to the right, use your whole upper body movement to lock out your opponent's arm.

IMPORTANT POINTS

- In point ③, grasp your opponent's hand and wrist without tensing your shoulders.

- In point ④, do not relax the Second Control joint lock on your opponent's arm.

- In order to get the most out of the movement of individual parts of your body, it is important to move your whole body (arms, legs, back etc.) in unison, and to achieve the correct spacing; something that is true for all Aikido techniques.

①

②

③

④

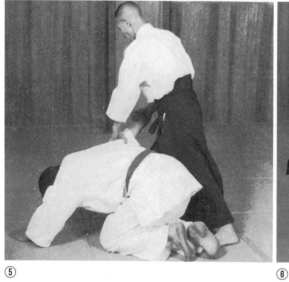

⑤

⑥

⑦

KATATE-MOCHI NIKAJO-OSAE 2 片手持ち二ヵ条抑え 2

Wrist Grasp; Second Control Type 2

① Stand facing your opponent in the basic stance, left foot forward. Your opponent stands right foot forward. Your opponent grasps your left wrist with his right hand and pushes.

② When your opponent pushes, slide diagonally to the left on your left foot, and aim a backhanded punch to your opponent's face with your right hand. Keeping your left shoulder down, thrust your left hand out to the left in a circular movement.

③ Bring both hands up and around in front of you in a big curve. Grasping your opponent's hand and wrist, slide your right foot back around behind you, so that you face your opponent from the side.

④ Apply the Second Control wrist lock as though you are cutting down with a sword.

⑤⑥ Without relaxing the wrist lock, cut downward in a spiral, spinning your arms, body, and right leg around clock-wise, pivoting on your left foot, and come to a stop on your left knee.

IMPORTANT POINTS

- In point ②, look at your opponent's face when you aim a backhanded punch at him.

- In point ③, when you spin your right foot and grasp your opponent's hand and wrist, remember to slide your foot, and not to allow your hips to rise.

- In point ④, when cutting down, do not rely on your arm strength alone to cut down. Put your whole body into it. Make especially sure that your back leg does not bend.

- In point ⑤, start cutting down and turning with your arms slightly before moving your leg. Apply the finishing Second Control arm lock (pin) as described in the previous throw.

①

②

③

④

⑤

⑥

Three against one.

WAZA O MIGAKU · 1

Polishing Your Techniques · 1

With training you will become able to use, for example, a stick in the same way as your hands to apply a technique.

When applying the Second Control, relax your upper body and hands. Use your legs and lower back as a lever to focus your whole body's strength.

Elbow Grasp; Second Control Type 1

① Stand facing your opponent, both of you in the basic stance, right foot forward. Your opponent grasps your shirt by your left elbow with his right hand and pulls.

② Using your opponent's pull, slide in a curve to your left, and at the same time aim a backhanded punch with your right hand to your opponent's face.

③ Push your opponent's right arm upward, by sliding your left wrist up over his elbow, and at the same time grasp the back of his right hand with your right palm, fixing it to your elbow.

④ Place your left elbow onto your opponent's right wrist joint. Apply the Second Control wrist lock, pushing down with your elbow.

⑤ Without relaxing the pressure on your opponent's arm, slide diagonally forward to your right leading with your right foot, and at the same time cutting down in the same direction with your left elbow and wrist, and turning your hips to the right.

⑥⑦ Grasp your opponent's elbow from above with your left hand, whilst sliding your left foot in toward your opponent's side. Slide forward with your right foot and kneel on your left knee. Finally, apply the finishing Second Control arm lock (pin).

IMPORTANT POINTS

- In point ④, your palm should be held toward your face, as though you are holding a mirror. When applying the Second Control technique, relax your shoulders, tense your lower back, and push down as though you are cutting down through your opponent's body with the side of your hand.

- In point ⑤, when you are cutting down, keep your opponent's hand fixed to your elbow.

- In point ⑦, when grasping your opponent's elbow from above, make sure the thumb of your left hand is on the inner side of his elbow (toward you).

- The final Second Control arm lock (pin) is the same as for all other Second Control throws.

①

②

③

④

⑤

⑥

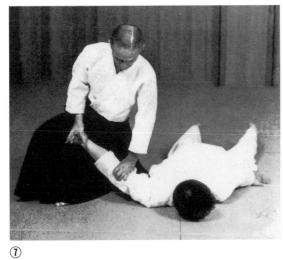

⑦

HIJI-MOCHI NIKAJO-OSAE 2　肘持ち二ヵ条抑え 2

Elbow Grasp; Second Control Type 2

① Stand facing your opponent in the basic stance, left foot forward. Your opponent stands right foot forward. With his right hand he grasps your shirt by your left elbow and pushes.

② Slide to your left and aim a backhanded punch at your opponent's face.

③ Pivoting on your left foot, spin your right foot slightly round behind you, so that you are facing your opponent from the side. At the same time, slide your opponent's right arm upward with your left wrist, and fix your elbow on top of his wrist joint.

④ Cut down with your left forearm, applying the Second Control wrist lock.

⑤ With your opponent's hand still attached to your elbow, cut down in a spiral with your left wrist, whilst pivoting on your left foot, and spinning your right foot around behind you.

⑥ Turn your upper body around one more half turn in the same direction, pushing your opponent flat to the floor.

IMPORTANT POINTS

- In point ③, the method of placing your elbow onto your opponent's wrist joint is exactly the same as in the Elbow Grasp; Second Control Type 1 throw.

- In point ⑤, from the position in the picture, remove your opponent's hand from your elbow while you are spinning around to the right. With your left hand grasp your opponent's elbow from above, turn your upper body around, and apply the finishing Second Control arm lock (pin).

①

②

③

④

⑤　　　　　　　　　　　　　　　　⑥

Gozo Shioda throws an opponent attacking from the rear out in front of him
and is immediately in position to cut him down with the blade.

KATA-MOCHI NIKAJO-OSAE 1　肩持ち二ヵ条抑え 1

Shoulder Grasp; Second Control Type 1

① You and your opponent stand facing each other, right foot forward. Your opponent grasps your shirt in front of your left shoulder with his right hand and pulls.

② Using your opponent's pull, slide to your left in a curve, and aim a backhanded punch at his face with your right hand.

③ Sliding back a little to the inside, thrust your left shoulder forward, and at the same time with your left wrist, push your opponent's elbow upward, lifting him off balance.

④ Drop your left forearm over your opponent's right arm, and grasp his wrist, fixing it to your shoulder.

⑤ Bend your right knee, putting your weight firmly on it, push your shoulder forward, and apply the Second Control wrist lock.

⑥ Without relaxing the wrist lock, and keeping your opponent's hand fixed to your shoulder, slide your left hand down from your opponent's wrist to grasp his elbow. Sliding diagonally forward on your right foot, push his elbow over to the front, and turn your hips to the right.

⑦ Slide your left foot into your opponent's side, thrusting forward with your left shoulder.

⑧ Slide forward with your right foot, forcing your opponent flat onto his stomach. Kneel with your left knee, and at the same time, remove your opponent's hand from your shoulder. Finally apply the finishing Second Control arm lock (pin).

IMPORTANT POINTS

- In point ③, when scraping against your opponent's elbow, pushing it upward and your opponent off balance, make sure your hips do not come into contact with your opponent.

- In point ⑤, when applying the Second Control wrist lock, keep your left hip pushed forward.

①

②

③

④

⑤

⑥

⑦

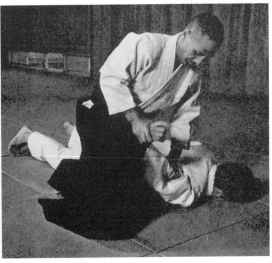
⑧

KATA-MOCHI NIKAJO-OSAE 2   肩持ち二ヵ条抑え 2

Shoulder Grasp; Second Control Type 2

① Stand facing your opponent, left foot forward. Your opponent stands right foot forward, and with his right hand, palm down, grasps your shirt in front of your left shoulder and pushes.

② Deflecting your opponent's push, slide to your left leading with your left foot, and at the same time aim a backhanded punch to your opponent's face with your right hand.

③ With your right hand, cover the back of your opponent's right hand with your palm and fix it to your shoulder. Pivoting on your left foot, spinning your right foot around behind you 45 degrees, push your opponent's elbow up with your left wrist.

④ Slide your left hand down to your opponent's wrist and, sliding forward on your left foot, apply the Second Control wrist lock.

⑤⑥ Pivot on your front (left) foot spinning your right foot around behind you 180 degrees. During the spin, remove your opponent's hand from your shoulder. Having finished the spin, turn your upper body round clockwise, lowering your body, so that you are facing the opposite direction, and kneel with your left knee.

⑦ Turn to face your opponent's body, and apply the finishing Second Control arm lock (pin).

①

②

③

④

⑤

⑥

⑦

SUWARI WAZA SHOMEN UCHI NIKAJO-OSAE 1　座り技正面打ち二ヵ条抑え 1

Kneeling Strike to the Forehead; Second Control Type 1

① Kneel opposite your opponent.

② With the side of your right hand strike at your opponent's forehead. With your left hand, make contact with your opponent's right elbow, and at the same time, get up onto your toes.

③ Slide diagonally forward to your right with your right knee, cutting down on your opponent's wrist and elbow in a circular movement.

④ Opening your legs slightly by sliding your left knee to the left, grasp your opponent's hand and wrist in preparation for applying the Second Control wrist lock.

⑤ Apply the Second Control wrist lock.

⑥ Keeping your opponent's wrist bent with your right hand, slide your left hand down to his elbow, and at the same time slide forward on your right knee.

⑦ Slide forward on your left knee, forcing your opponent further down.

⑧ Slide forward on your right knee, laying your opponent completely flat on his stomach.

⑨ Turn to face your opponent and apply the finishing Second Control arm lock (pin).

⑩⑪⑫ These photos show the method of grasping your opponent's wrist and hand, in preparation for applying the Second Control wrist lock.

IMPORTANT POINTS

- When you strike at your opponent, do not allow your hips to rise.

①

②

③

④

⑩

⑪

⑤

⑫

⑥ ⑦

⑧ ⑨

Gozo Shioda, checking his opponent as he goes to stab at his chest.

SHOMEN UCHI NIKAJO-OSAE 2　正面打ち二ヵ条抑え 2

Strike to the Forehead; Second Control Type 2

① Stand facing your opponent, left foot forward. Your opponent stands right foot forward and strikes at your forehead with the side of his right hand. When he does this, meet his elbow with your left hand, and thrust out your right wrist, blocking his strike and forcing him up and off balance.

② Allow your opponent's momentum to carry him forward and further off balance by pivoting on your left foot, spinning your right foot around behind you, leading your opponent around.

③ Slide the thumb of your right hand around your opponent's right wrist to grasp his hand, and at the same time, slide your left hand from his elbow to his wrist, grasping it in preparation for the Second Control wrist lock.

④ Apply the Second Control wrist lock.

⑤ Without relaxing the lock on your opponent's arm, force your opponent's arm downward in a spiral, whilst at the same time pivoting on your left foot, spinning your right foot around behind you 180 degrees. Transferring your weight from your left foot to your right foot, turn your upper body around a further 180 degrees, lowering your body and kneeling on your left knee. Apply the finishing Second Control arm lock (pin).

①

②

③

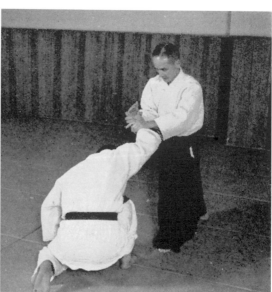

④

⑤

- Pivoting on one foot is considered a difficult technique generally, but in this throw, you have to be especially careful not to pull with your arms, as this will cause you to put too much strength into your upper body, disrupting your overall balance, and preventing you from using your arms, legs, and hips in unison. In order to overcome this difficulty, keep a correct posture, pivot over your center of gravity, cut downward with your arms, spin your hips, and then transfer your weight from your left foot to your right foot.

June 11th 1966. Combined Martial Arts Competition. Gozo Shioda sidesteps his opponent's stab at the last split second, and sends him flying with a well timed blow.

SANKAJO-OSAE 三ヵ条抑え
Third Control

Third Control is the name given to the technique where you bend your opponent's arm into a backward letter "C" shape, lock his wrist, elbow, and shoulder joint, and force him face down on the floor.

SANKAJO-SHIME NO KATA 三ヵ条締めの形
The Various Forms of the Third Control Technique

Although there is a great number and variety of moves in Aikido, in principle there are only two types of movement—where you turn your body, and when you push forward. In Aikido the golden rule is: If you are pushed, turn. If you are pulled, go forward in a curve.

SHOMEN-UCHI (ZENSHIN) 正面打ち（前進）
From a Strike to the Forehead (When Advancing)

From the position where, having aimed a blow at your opponent's forehead and forced him down, in the same way as in the Strike to the Forehead; First Control Type 1 throw, slide your right hand from your opponent's wrist to grasp his fingers. Slide forward on your right foot, thrusting your opponent's arm forward in a circular movement, forcing his palm round to the front. Remove your left hand from your opponent's elbow and, trapping his wrist joint between your thumb and forefinger, grasp the palm of your opponent's right hand (from the side of his little finger) with your remaining three fingers. Turn your opponent's wrist over so that the back of your left hand is facing upward, and press down on your opponent's elbow joint with your right hand. Slide forward with your left foot, then right foot, and apply the final Third Control arm lock (pin).

①

②

③

④

SHOMEN-UCHI (KAITEN)
正面打ち（回転）

From a Strike to the Forehead (When Pivoting)

When your opponent aims a blow to your forehead, spin around to the rear, allowing your opponent's momentum to carry him forward and unbalance him. Grasp his fingers with your right hand and thrust them upward in a circular movement. Remove your left hand from your opponent's elbow and trap the wrist joint of his right hand between your thumb and forefinger, and grasp the palm of your opponent's right hand (from the side of his little finger) with your remaining three fingers. Hold your opponent's hand up to your shoulder level, thrusting it toward his armpit, and lock out his arm. Keep your left hand (holding your opponent's hand in the Third Control) right in front of you, and apply the lock without changing the position of your left hand. Furthermore, do not use your arm strength to twist your opponent's hand, but rotate your whole body to apply the arm lock.

①

②

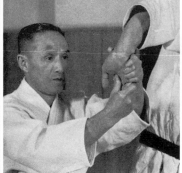

③

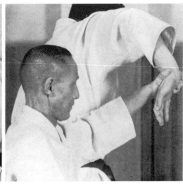

④

USHIRO RYOTE-MOCHI (TEKUBI-DORI)　後ろ両手持ち（手首取り）

From a Double Wrist Grasp from behind—where you grasp your opponent's wrist.

When your opponent grasps both of your wrists from behind, bring both hands up over your head to lift your opponent up and off balance. As you lower your hands with your right hand (your right wrist still being held by your opponent) grasp your opponent's left hand. Using your left hand as a base, thrust both your hands in a circular movement in the direction of your opponent's left armpit, locking out his arm. Make sure you do not over-extend or pull in your arms. Keeping the same spacing between you and your opponent, and using your body as a fulcrum, apply the arm lock by pivoting.

①

②

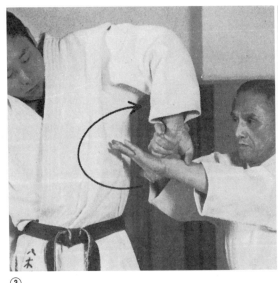

③

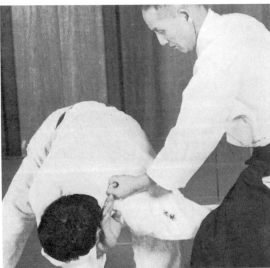

④

SANKAJO NO OSAE-KATA 三ヵ条の抑え方
Application of the Third Control Finishing Arm Lock (Pin)

You will find explanations of throws using the Third Control in the following pages. Here the finishing Third Control arm lock (pin) is explained. As it is the same for all Third Control throws, it is important to fully master this technique.

① This is the position where you have forced your opponent flat onto his stomach.

② Turn your body to face your opponent's head and shoulders, and at the same time cover your left hand, which is holding your opponent's hand, with your right hand.

③ Without relaxing the arm lock, grasp your opponent's hand with your right hand and fix his palm to your chest.

④ Place the side of your left hand against your opponent's elbow.

⑤ Turn your hips to change the direction of your upper body and lock your opponent's arm.

①

②

③

④

⑤

SHOMEN UCHI SANKAJO-OSAE 1　正面打ち三ヵ条抑え 1
Strike to the Forehead; Third Control Type 1

①② In the same manner as the Strike to the Forehead; First Control Type 1 throw, strike at your opponent's forehead. Then, advancing to your right, cut down, forcing him to the floor.

③ Slide your right hand from your opponent's wrist down to grasp his fingers. Slide forward on your right foot, thrusting your opponent's arm forward in a circular movement, forcing his palm round to the front.

④ Grasp your opponent's right hand with your left hand and, pressing down on his elbow joint from above with your right hand, slide in toward your opponent with your left foot.

⑤ Take one more sliding step with your right foot, and kneel on your left knee. Apply the finishing Third Control arm lock (pin).

IMPORTANT POINTS

▪ In point ③, when you grasp your opponent's fingers with your right hand and thrust them forward in a circular movement, make sure you push them forward, not upward, and at the same time, slide forward without relaxing the pressure on his elbow with your left hand.

▪ In point ④, when you change the grip on your opponent's hand from your right hand to your left hand, make sure not to relax the pressure pushing forward on your opponent's arm. When sliding forward on your left foot, keep both hands (in the Third Control position) and both feet over the same line.

▪ In point ⑤, bring your left knee down without relaxing the Third Control arm lock.

①

②

③

④

⑤

SHOMEN UCHI SANKAJO-OSAE 2　正面打ち三ヵ条抑え 2
Strike to the Forehead; Third Control Type 2

① Stand facing your opponent in the basic stance, left foot forward. Your opponent stands right foot forward, and strikes at your forehead with the side of his right hand. When he does this, block his strike using both hands. In order to lift your opponent off balance, thrust his elbow upward with your left hand, and at the same time, block his strike with the inside of your right wrist, forcing the momentum of his blow upward.

② Allow your opponent's momentum to carry him forward and off balance by pivoting on your left foot, spinning around to face the opposite direction.

③ With your right hand grasp the fingers of your opponent's right hand. With your left hand grasp your opponent's elbow, and thrust it upward in a circular movement.

④ Grasp your opponent's right hand with your left hand, in preparation for applying the Third Control arm lock. Pivot on your left foot (front foot) swinging your right foot in a curve anti-clockwise. As you turn your hips to the left, keep your Third Control grasp on your opponent's hand, twisting it in the direction of his right armpit, locking out his arm.

⑤ Slide your left foot (front foot) around behind you, lowering your center of gravity, and cut downward on your opponent's arm without relaxing the arm lock. With your right hand, aim a punch to your opponent's face.

⑥ Slide a little further to the rear, left foot first, and then, taking an angle of over 90 degrees to the right, slide forward on your right foot, bringing your left knee to the floor. Apply the finishing Third Control arm lock (pin).

IMPORTANT POINTS

- In point ③, when you thrust your opponent's arm upward, make sure that your hand holding his elbow is also thrust upward.

- In point ④, spin your right foot around anti-clockwise, turn your hips to the left, and apply the Third Control arm lock all at the same time. (Do not rely on your arm strength, but use the force generated by spinning, so make sure that your whole body rotates in unison.)

①

②

③

④

⑤

⑥

JAPANESE NAME: SUWARI WAZA SHOMEN UCHI SANKAJO OSAE 2

座り技正面打ち三ヵ条抑え 2

English Name: Kneeling Strike to the Forehead; Third Control Type 2

This throw is carried out in the same way as the standing version. It is especially important, however, to ensure that your knees do not rise up off the floor. There is also a tendency for each movement to become too small, so you must pay more attention to the way your shift your weight and keep the spacing between you and your opponent. If you change the word "foot" from the standing version to "knee", all the moves remain the same.

The only slight difference comes in the finishing Third Control arm lock (pin). Whereas in throws that start from the standing position you kneel on one knee only, in throws that start from the kneeling position you kneel on both knees.

IMPORTANT POINTS

With throws that start from the kneeling position, moving becomes more difficult. It is easy for the spacing between you and your opponent to become cramped, or for your legs to get out of position, so pay special attention to these aspects.

①

②

Gozo Shioda, grasping his opponent's shirt, brings him off balance and drops him in a split second.

③

④

⑤

⑥

⑦

WAZA O MIGAKU · 2
Polishing Your Techniques · 2

It is of vital importance to move your hands, feet and hips in unison to perform techniques.

When applying the Third Control arm lock, always keep your arms on your own body's center line.

KATATE-MOCHI SANKAJO-OSAE 1　片手持ち三ヵ条抑え 1

Wrist Grasp; Third Control Type 1

① You and your opponent stand facing each other, right foot forward. When your opponent grasps your left wrist and pulls, slide to your left and aim a backhanded punch to his face with your right hand.

② Using the same technique as for the Wrist Grasp; First Control Type 1 throw, focus on your opponent's thumb, sliding forward on your right foot, and bringing your hands up in a large curve, to lift him off balance.

③ Leading with the side of your left hand, cut downward.

④ Slide forward once more with your right foot, pressing down on your opponent's elbow, forcing him down further.

⑤ Remove your left hand from your opponent's elbow, and grasp his hand with the Third Control grip. Take your right hand from his wrist, and grasp his elbow.

⑥ Without relaxing the Third Control arm lock, slide your left foot in toward your opponent's armpit, thrusting his arm in the same direction.

⑦⑧ Slide your right foot forward, bringing your left knee to the floor. Apply the finishing Third Control arm lock (pin).

IMPORTANT POINTS

▪ In point ②, bring your hands up as though your elbows are the pivotal point of a fan. Make sure to keep your elbows down. Also, make sure your opponent's thumb stays tightly stuck to your wrist.

①

②

③

④

⑤

⑥

⑦

⑧

KATATE-MOCHI SANKAJO-OSAE 2　片手持ち三ヵ条抑え 2
Wrist Grasp; Third Control Type 2

① Stand facing your opponent in the basic stance, left foot forward. Your opponent stands right foot forward. As he grasps your left wrist with his right hand and pushes, using the same technique as for the Wrist Grasp; First Control Type 2 throw, slide to the side and aim a backhanded punch to his face.

② Pivoting on your left foot and rotating your right foot slightly to the rear, lift your opponent up and off balance.

③ Pivoting on your left foot again, sweeping your right foot around clockwise behind you, cut down with the side of your left hand.

④ In order to unbalance your opponent even more, pivot again, pressing down on his elbow joint. Then, switch your left and right hand over and assume the Third Control grip.

⑤ Slide your front foot (left foot) around behind you, cutting down with your left hand and aiming a backhanded punch with your right hand to your opponent's face.

⑥ Slide one more step to the rear, then turn to your right and slide forward with your right foot.

⑦ Bring your left knee down to the floor, and apply the finishing Third Control arm lock (pin).

IMPORTANT POINTS

- Take care not to fall into the common mistake with throws that start from a Wrist Grasp of focusing too heavily on your opponent's hand, and forgetting to bring the whole of his body off balance.

①

②

③

④

⑤

⑥

⑦

KATA-MOCHI SANKAJO-OSAE 1 　肩持ち三ヵ条抑え 1

Shoulder Grasp; Third Control Type 1

① You and your opponent stand facing each other, right foot forward. Your opponent grasps your shirt in front of your left shoulder and pulls. Use your opponent's pull to slide to your left in a circular movement, and aim a backhanded punch to his face with your right hand.

② Thrusting your left shoulder forward, push your opponent's elbow upward by sliding your left wrist up against it, bringing the side of your left hand around to the front.

③ Slide forward on your right foot, square your hips, and cut downward with your left hand.

④ Sliding forward one more step on your right foot, remove your opponent's hand from your shoulder.

⑤ Grasp his hand in the Third Control grip.

⑥⑦ Slide forward with your left foot, then your right foot, bringing your left knee to the floor. Apply the finishing Third Control arm lock (pin).

IMPORTANT POINTS

- Never give your opponent a chance to recover his balance.
- Do not lean forward in order to cut your opponent down. Instead, keep your posture straight and lower your center of gravity to push down on your opponent.

①

②

③

④

⑤

⑥

⑦

KATA-MOCHI SANKAJO-OSAE 2　肩持ち三ヵ条抑え 2

Shoulder Grasp; Third Control Type 2

① Stand facing your opponent, left foot forward. Your opponent stands right foot forward. When he grasps your shirt in front of your left shoulder and pushes, slide to your left and aim a backhanded punch to his face with your right hand. Then grasp the back of your opponent's right hand, covering it with the palm of your right hand.

② Thrusting your left shoulder forward, push your opponent's elbow upward by sliding your left wrist up against it, forcing your opponent up and off balance.

③ Pivoting on your left foot, rotating your right leg around behind you clockwise, cut downward in a spiral with the side of your left hand, forcing your opponent to the floor.

④ Rotating once more in the same direction, remove your opponent's hand from your shoulder.

⑤ Change your hands over to grasp his right hand with your left hand using the Third Control grip. Slide your front foot (left foot) round behind you, and aim a punch to his face with your right hand.

⑥⑦ With your right hand push down on your opponent's elbow joint. Slide backward one more step, then, turning to your right, slide forward bringing your left knee to the floor. Apply the finishing Third Control arm lock (pin).

IMPORTANT POINTS

- Pay special attention to the spacing between you and your opponent. When cutting down with the side of your left hand, avoid pulling. Pulling your opponent will lead to the spacing becoming cramped, and your spin becoming too tight. This is likely to cause you to shift your weight to your back foot, unbalancing you instead of your opponent.

①

②

③

④

⑤

⑥

⑦

USHIRO RYOTE-MOCHI SANKAJO-OSAE 1 後ろ両手持ち三ヵ条抑え 1
Double Wrist Grasp from Behind; Third Control Type 1

① Your opponent comes round behind you and grasps both your wrists and pulls.

② Bend your wrists and lower your center of gravity. Slide your left foot slightly out to the left, removing the power from your opponent's pull and getting your back out of the line of your opponent's chest, creating a favorable position to deal with your opponent's grip.

③ Having bent your wrists, now thrust both your hands out in the direction of your fingertips. Bring both hands up over your head in an egg-shaped curve, so that your opponent is forced up onto his toes.

④ Pull your right foot out behind you in a curve so that it comes outside of the line of your left foot. At the same time, lower your hands to your chest height, and grasp your opponent's left hand using the Third Control grip.

⑤ Pivoting on the toes of both feet, turn your hips to the right, shifting your weight onto your right foot, and facing right. At the same time thrust with both hands in the direction of your opponent's left armpit, applying the Third Control arm lock.

⑥ Sliding your right leg behind you, cut down with your right hand, and aim a punch to your opponent's face with your left hand.

⑦⑧ Pushing down on your opponent's elbow with your left hand, leading with your right foot, slide backward in the direction your opponent's arm is pointing. Turning to your left, slide forward on your left foot, bringing your right knee to the floor. Apply the finishing Third Control arm lock (pin).

IMPORTANT POINTS

- Bringing both hands up over your head when your opponent is grasping your wrists is an exceptionally difficult technique. A lot of practice will be required in order to master it.

①

②

①②③ You and your opponent stand facing each other, right foot forward. After completing the preliminary exercise for throws where your opponent attacks you from behind, your opponent comes round behind you, grasps both your wrists, and pushes.

④⑤ Using your opponent's push, slide your front foot forward slightly, and thrust both hands out in front of you. Then raise your hands up over your head in a curve, as though sliding your hands over a large egg.

⑥⑦ Pivot on your right foot, rotating your left foot around clockwise in front of you 180 degrees. With your right hand, grasp your opponent's left hand using the Third Control grip.

⑧⑨ Rotate a little further to lock out your opponent's arm.

⑩ Bringing your right hand down and your right foot back in a curve, at the same time aim a punch to your opponent's face with your left hand.

⑪ Grasp your opponent's elbow from above with your left hand. Slide backward one more step on your right foot, forcing your opponent to the floor.

⑫ Taking an angle of over 90 degrees, slide left with your left foot, bringing your right knee down, and your opponent flat onto his stomach.

⑬⑭ Turn swiftly to face your opponent and change your hold on your opponent's hand and arm to apply the finishing Third Control arm lock (pin).

①

②

③

④

⑤

⑥

YONKAJO-OSAE 四ヵ条抑え

Fourth Control

Fourth Control is the name given to the technique where you focus your strength into the base of your index finger, pressing it into the pressure point in the inner side of your opponent's wrist near his pulse. When applied correctly, this will cause a sharp pain in your opponent's arm, quickly incapacitating him.

KATATE-MOCHI YONKAJO-OSAE 1 片手持ち四ヵ条抑え 1
Wrist Grasp; Fourth Control Type 1

In this throw, you use the Fourth Control grip to subdue your opponent when he grasps your wrist and pulls.

① You and your opponent stand facing each other, right foot forward. Your opponent grasps your left wrist with his right hand, pulling slightly.

② Use your opponent's pull to slide sideways to your left. At the same time aim a backhanded punch with your right hand to his face.

③ Bring your left hand back in front of you, sliding forward slightly, and at the same time grasp the back of your opponent's wrist with your right hand, bending his arm into a right angle at the elbow and thrusting upward.

④ Slide forward on your right foot and at the same time cut down with your hands. For the Fourth Control grip to be effective, your hands should be directly in front of you.

⑤ Slide your left foot in toward your opponent's armpit, keeping the Fourth Control grip tight on your opponent's wrist.

⑥ Slide forward on your right foot and bring your left knee down to the floor, turning your hips to the right and forcing your opponent flat onto his stomach.

⑦ Change your grip on your opponent's wrist to apply the finishing arm lock (pin), which is exactly the same as the Second Control finishing arm lock (pin).

⑧⑨ These photos show how to grasp your opponent's wrist using the Fourth Control grip.

IMPORTANT POINTS

- Bend you opponent's arm and grip his wrist. Gripping tightly with your little finger, press the base of your index finger to the inner side of his wrist. Do not try to twist your opponent's arm using your arm strength.

① ② ③

④

⑤

⑥

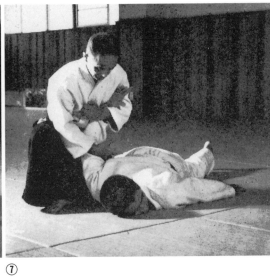

⑦

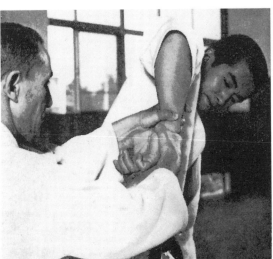

⑧

⑨

In this throw, you use the Fourth Control grip to subdue your opponent when he grasps your wrist and pushes.

① Stand facing your opponent in the basic stance, left foot forward. Your opponent stands right foot forward, grasps your left wrist with his right hand, and pushes.

② Using your opponent's push, slide to your left and aim a backhanded punch to his face.

③ Turning your opponent's wrist over, grasp it using the Fourth Control grip, and thrust upward.

④ Pivoting on your left foot, sweep your right foot around clockwise behind you, and cut down in a spiral forcing your

opponent to the floor, keeping the Fourth Control grip tight on his wrist.

⑤ Slide your right (back) foot forward, thrusting with your hips, and laying your opponent flat onto the floor.

⑥ Apply the finishing arm lock (pin) in the same way as described in the Wrist Grasp; Fourth Control Type 1 throw.

IMPORTANT POINTS

- In point ④, make sure you keep your opponent's arm bent.

①

②

③

④

Gozo Shioda, focusing his strength into his big toe to throw his opponent.

⑤   ⑥

SHOMEN UCHI YONKAJO-OSAE 1　正面打ち四ヵ条抑え 1

Strike to the Forehead; Fourth Control Type 1

① You and your opponent stand facing each other, right foot forward.

②③ In the same manner as the Strike to the Forehead; First Control Type 1 throw, strike at your opponent's forehead with the side of your right hand, and with your left hand make contact with your opponent's elbow. Push upward in an arc and then, advancing to your right, cut down.

④ Slide your left hand from your opponent's elbow down to grasp his wrist in the Fourth Control grip.

⑤ Slide forward with your right foot, and push your hips forward to apply pressure to the pressure point in your opponent's wrist.

⑥ Slide your left foot in toward your opponent's armpit, forcing him down further.

⑦ Bring your right foot forward, squaring your hips, to lay your opponent flat on his stomach.

⑧ Apply the finishing arm lock (pin) as per the Second Control technique.

①

②

③

④

⑤   ⑥

⑦

⑧

SHOMEN UCHI YONKAJO-OSAE 2　正面打ち四ヵ条抑え 2
Strike to the Forehead; Fourth Control Type 2

① Stand facing your opponent in the basic stance, left foot forward. Your opponent stands right foot forward.

② Your opponent strikes at your forehead with the side of his right hand. Block his strike using the inside of your right wrist in the same way as in the First Control; Strike to the Forehead Type 2 throw.

③ Allow your opponent's momentum to carry him forward by pivoting on your left foot, spinning your right foot around behind you clockwise.

④ With your left hand grasp your opponent's wrist in the Fourth Control grip. Rotate your right foot around behind

again clockwise, to apply pressure to the pressure point in your opponent's wrist.

⑤ Pivoting once again on your left foot, swing your right foot around behind you and cut down with your hands in a spiral to force your opponent down and off balance.

⑥ Slide forward on your right foot, squaring your hips, and forcing your opponent flat onto his stomach.

⑦ Apply the finishing arm lock (pin) as in the Type 1 throw.

①　②

③

④

⑤

⑥

⑦

Gozo Shioda, grasping his opponent's shirt, brings him off balance and drops him in a split second.

KATA-MOCHI YONKAJO-OSAE 1　肩持ち四ヵ条抑え 1
Shoulder Grasp; Fourth Control Type 1

① You and your opponent stand facing each other, right foot forward. Your opponent grasps the shirt in front of your left shoulder (with his right hand, palm down) and pulls.

② Slide diagonally to your left, and aim a backhanded punch to your opponent's face with your right hand.

③ In the same way as in the Shoulder Grasp; First Control Type 1 throw, slide forward on your right foot, thrusting your left shoulder forward, and push your opponent's elbow upward by sliding your left wrist up against it.

④ Keeping your opponent's hand fixed to your shoulder, slide forward on your right foot, square your hips, and cut downward with the side of your left hand.

⑤ Sliding forward one more step on your right foot, remove your opponent's hand from your shoulder.

⑥ Grasp your opponent's wrist using the Fourth Control grip. Keep your grip on the back of your opponent's hand with your right hand, and place the base of the index finger of your left hand on the inside of his wrist, thumb side, over his pulse. (Enlarged photo.)

⑦ Slide your left foot toward your opponent's armpit, applying pressure to the pressure point in your opponent's wrist.

⑧ Slide your right foot forward, squaring your hips, forcing your opponent flat onto his stomach. Apply the finishing arm lock (pin) as per the Second Control technique.

①

②

③

④

⑤

⑥-1

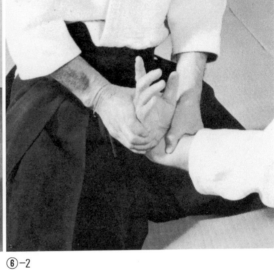

⑥-2

⑦

⑧

KATA-MOCHI YONKAJO-OSAE 2 肩持ち四ヵ条抑え 2
Shoulder Grasp; Fourth Control Type 2

① Stand facing your opponent, left foot forward. Your opponent stands right foot forward. He grasps your shirt in front of your left shoulder and pushes.

② Using your opponent's push, slide diagonally to your left and aim a backhanded punch to his face with your right hand, forcing your opponent off balance.

③ In the same way as in the Shoulder Grasp; Third Control Type 2 throw, rotate your right leg around behind you and push your opponent's elbow upward by sliding your left wrist up against it.

④ With your opponent's hand fixed to your shoulder, pivot on your left foot, rotating your right leg around behind you clockwise, and cut downward in a spiral with the side of your left hand, forcing your opponent to the floor.

⑤ Rotating once more in the same direction, remove your opponent's hand from your shoulder.

⑥ Grasp your opponent's wrist with your left hand using the Fourth Control grip.

⑦ Pivoting on your left foot, spin your right foot around behind you clockwise, and raise your hands up, forcing your opponent up as you apply pressure to the pressure point in his wrist.

⑧ Without relaxing the Fourth Control grip on your opponent's wrist, cut downward in a spiral, sweeping your right foot around clockwise in a big circle, pushing from your hips to put all your body weight behind your movement.

⑨ Slide your back foot (right foot) forward and bring your left knee to the floor, squaring your hips.

⑩ Apply the finishing arm lock (pin) in the same way as in the Type 1 throw.

①

②

③

④

⑤

⑥

⑦

⑧

⑨

⑩

IRIMI-NAGE　入身投げ
Body Check Throw

There are two forms of Body Check Throw—the Frontal Body Check Throw and the Side Body Check Throw. In the Frontal Body Check Throw, you redirect your opponent's momentum before sliding up inside his defenses and throwing him. In the Side Body Check Throw, you deflect your opponent's strength and approach him side-on before throwing him.

YOKOMEN UCHI SHOMEN IRIMI-NAGE 1　横面打ち正面入身投げ 1
Strike to the Side of the Head; Frontal Body Check Type 1

① You and your opponent stand facing each other, right foot forward.

② Your opponent strikes at the side of your head with the side of his right hand. Slide diagonally forward to your left, and block your opponent's strike with the side of your left wrist, aiming a backhanded punch to his face with your right hand at the same time.

③ Place your right wrist over your left forearm, trapping your opponent's arm in a cross.

④ Turn your hips clockwise, letting your opponent's momentum carry his hand forward.

⑤ Take a large sliding step forward on your left foot to the rear of your opponent, and at the same time, sweep your right hand up to your opponent's throat in a thrusting movement. Push your right shoulder and hips forward, and place your weight firmly over your left foot. With your left hand, grasp the back of your opponent's collar.

⑥ Thrusting your right shoulder and hips forward, push diagonally downward with your right hand, turning it over so that the palm is down, and slide diagonally behind your opponent with your right foot.

⑦ Having thrown your opponent, straighten your posture.

IMPORTANT POINTS

- When throwing your partner, make sure your lower body and your upper body move forward at the same time.

①

②

③

④

⑤-1

⑤-2

⑥

⑦

SUWARI WAZA YOKOMEN UCHI SHOMEN IRIMI-NAGE 2

座り技横面打ち正面入身投げ 2

Kneeling Strike to the Side of the Head; Frontal Body Check Type 2

① You and your opponent stand facing each other, right foot forward, before kneeling.

② Your opponent strikes to the side of your head. Slide diagonally to your left on your knees, and block the blow with the inside of your left wrist, and with your right hand aim a backhanded punch to your opponent's face.

③ Place your right wrist over your left forearm, making a cross and trapping your opponent's right wrist.

④⑤ Bring both wrists (trapping your opponent's wrist) around and cut down in a spiral so that your opponent falls forward and off balance. Pivot on your left knee, rotating your right knee around behind you clockwise, allowing your opponent's momentum to carry him forward. Grasp the back of his collar with your left hand and transfer your weight to your right knee.

⑥ Punch to your opponent's face with your right hand and, as your opponent flinches to avoid the punch, shift your weight back to your left knee and bring your right hand up past his throat. Using your whole body, throw your opponent backward.

⑦ Having thrown your opponent, straighten your posture.

IMPORTANT POINTS

- In point ④, do not grasp your opponent's wrist with your right hand. Grasping the wrist will lead you to pull your opponent's arm, making it easy for you to lose your balance. Strive to sweep your opponent up, by rotating in a wide circle, and letting his momentum carry him forward.

①

②

③

④

⑤

⑥-1

⑥-2

⑦

Strike to the Side of the Head; Frontal Body Check Type 2

① Stand facing your opponent in the basic stance, left foot forward. Your opponent stands right foot forward, and strikes at your left temple with the side of his right hand. As your opponent raises his hands to strike, raise your own hands and, sliding diagonally forward to your left, block the strike with your left wrist. At the same time, aim a backhanded punch to your opponent's face with your right hand.

② Place your right wrist over your left forearm, trapping your opponent's arm in a cross.

③④⑤ Sliding your right wrist back past your left hand, pivot on your left foot, sweeping your right leg around behind you 180 degrees. Part of the way through your spin, bring your left hand up to the back of your opponent's collar.

⑥ After rotating 180 degrees, turn your hips to the right, shifting your body weight to your right foot, in a movement identical to that in Body Line Exercise Type 2, so that your opponent is off balance and falling forward.

⑦⑧⑨ Aim a punch with your right hand to your opponent's face. As your opponent flinches backward to avoid the punch, slide your right hand up from his chest to his throat, thrusting him upward, and at the same time, turn around to face the opposite direction by placing your weight back onto your left foot, forcing your opponent to bend over backward.

⑩ Slide your back (right) foot diagonally to the right behind your opponent, throwing him onto his back, keeping your weight and momentum pushing forward.

①

②

③

④

⑤

⑥

⑦

⑧

⑨

⑩

SUWARI WAZA KATATE-MOCHI SOKUMEN IRIMI-NAGE 1

座り技片手持ち側面入身投げ 1

Kneeling Wrist Grasp; Side Body Check Type 1

① You and your opponent stand facing each other, right foot forward, before kneeling. Your opponent grasps your left wrist and pulls.

② Using your opponent's pull, and pushing with your left hip to increase the strength in your left hand and left knee, open the fingers of your left hand strongly, and pivot slightly on your left knee, so that your body is facing a little to the right, causing your opponent to lose his balance.

③④ Slide diagonally forward on your left knee and at the same time force your opponent to lean over backward by sliding the back of your left hand up to his throat and your right hand to the side of his chest.

⑤⑥ Slide forward once more on your left knee, throwing your opponent onto his back, keeping your weight and momentum pushing forward.

①

②

③

④

⑤

⑥

KATATE-MOCHI SOKUMEN IRIMI-NAGE 1　片手持ち側面入身投げ 1
Wrist Grasp; Side Body Check Type 1

① You and your opponent stand facing each other, right foot forward. Your opponent grasps your left wrist with his right hand and pulls. (photo omitted.)

② Using your opponent's pull, slide your right foot to just in front of your opponent's front foot, your toes pointing right, so that your opponent's foot and your foot together combine to make a "T" shape. Drop your left hip, and putting your weight into both your hands, with your left hand above your right hand, force your opponent off balance.

③④ Take a large sliding step with your left foot past your opponent, and at the same time thrust upward with your left hand, bringing the side of your right hand up against your opponent's stomach, and your waist tightly against his, forcing him to bend over backward.

⑤ Squaring your hips, slide forward with your left foot, and cut downward with the back of your left hand, throwing your opponent onto his back.

IMPORTANT POINTS

- In point ②, it is fine for the heel of your back foot to be raised. Make sure you press down strongly with the toes of both feet. Do not stick your hips out.

- In point ③, do not simply stand up, but push forward strongly.

- In point ⑤, Put your weight on your left foot, keep your back leg straight, keep your hips down, and keep your weight and momentum pushing forward.

②

③

④

⑤

① Stand facing your opponent, left foot forward. Your opponent stands right foot forward. He grasps your left wrist and pushes.

② In the same way as in Body Movement Exercise Type 2, pivot on your left foot, allowing your opponent's momentum to carry him forward so that you are facing his side.

③ As your opponent tries to recover his balance and stand up straight, bring your left wrist up in a circular movement, sliding forward on your left foot, thrusting your opponent up and off balance backward.

④ Cut down with your hands in the same way as in the Wrist Grasp; Side Body Check Type 1 Throw.

IMPORTANT POINTS

- When moving, always slide your feet.

①

②

③

③

④

KATA-MOCHI SOKUMEN IRIMI-NAGE 1　肩持ち側面入身投げ 1

Shoulder Grasp; Side Body Check Type 1

In this throw when your opponent grasps your shirt and pulls, you slide into your opponent from the side and throw him onto his back.

① You and your opponent stand facing each other, right foot forward. Your opponent grasps the shirt in front of your left shoulder with his right hand and pulls.

② Place your left wrist over your opponent's right arm, and combining with his pull, cut down and to the right with the side of your wrist. Turning your hips to the right, force your opponent off balance.

③ As your opponent tries to recover, slide your left foot in behind him, and force him to bend over backward.

④ Squaring your hips, bring your left arm down and, with your right hand making contact with your opponent's stomach, throw him onto his back.

⑤ This photo shows point ② in more detail. Note the position of both your hands, your opponent's arm, and the way your opponent is forced off balance.

IMPORTANT POINTS

- Place your left wrist over your opponent's arm from the outside, and using his pull, turn your hips. As your opponent tries to straighten up, slide in closer to him, so that your waist comes into contact with his right hip.

③

④

①

②

⑤

KATA-MOCHI SOKUMEN IRIMI-NAGE 2 　肩持ち側面入身投げ 2
Shoulder Grasp; Side Body Check Type 2

In this throw, when your opponent grasps your shirt and pushes, you deflect his push and come at him from the side before throwing him onto his back.

① Stand facing your opponent in the basic stance, left foot forward. Your opponent stands right foot forward and grasps your shirt in front of your left shoulder with his right hand and pushes.

② Using your opponent's push, pivot on your left foot, rotating your right foot around clockwise.

③ As your opponent tries to straighten up, bring your arms up and around, sliding forward to thrust your opponent's body upward.

④⑤ Cut down and throw your opponent in the same way as in the Shoulder Grasp; Side Body Check Type 1 Throw.

IMPORTANT POINTS

- Apply the side of your wrist to your opponent's arm from the outside and, utilizing your opponent's push, bring your hand around.

①

②

③

④

⑤

Gozo Shioda, as his opponent goes to grasp his left elbow, uses a Body Check and brings his opponent off balance.

YOKOMEN UCHI SOKUMEN IRIMI-NAGE 1　横面打ち側面入身投げ 1

Strike to the Side of the Head; Side Body Check Type 1

① You and your opponent stand facing each other, right foot forward.

② Your opponent strikes at the side of your head with the side of his right hand. Sliding diagonally to your left, block the strike with your left wrist, unbalancing your opponent, and aim a backhanded punch to his face with your right hand.

③ Trap your opponent's right wrist by crossing your right wrist over your left forearm.

④⑤ Slide your right foot to a point just in front of your opponent's front foot, with your toes pointing to the outside, so your opponent's foot and your foot combine to make a letter "T" shape, and turn your hips to the right. With your right hand, cut diagonally downward in a curve to the right, and bring the elbow of your left arm from underneath to thrust upward to your opponent's throat, pushing him off balance.

⑥ Sliding forward on your left foot, thrust your left hand

out. Bring the side of your right hand up against your opponent's stomach. Bring your waist up tightly against your opponent's waist, and push him further off balance.

⑦ Thrusting forward with your hips, slide forward on your left foot, cutting downward with both hands. Having thrown your opponent, straighten out your posture.

IMPORTANT POINTS

- In point ②, when you block your opponent's strike, lower your stance, and do not lift your shoulder.

- In point ④, keep your stance low. Do not grasp your opponent's wrist with your right hand.

- In point ⑥, when you thrust out your left hand, do not raise your shoulder.

- When you throw your opponent, do not throw to the side. Cut downward as you move forward, like a wave.

①

②

③

④

⑤

⑥

⑦

YOKOMEN UCHI SOKUMEN IRIMI-NAGE 2　横面打ち側面入身投げ 2

Strike to the Side of the Head, Side Body Check Type 2

① Stand facing your opponent in the basic stance, left foot forward. Your opponent stands right foot forward.

②③ When your opponent raises his hands above his head in preparation to strike at the side of your head, raise your own hands above your head. Slide diagonally forward to your left, and block your opponent's strike with the side of your left wrist, and at the same time aim a punch to his face with the back of your right hand.

④⑤⑥ Place your right wrist over your left forearm, trapping your opponent's arm in a cross. Sliding your right hand

back to the right, lower your stance a little and, pushing your opponent off balance, get into position to perform the Side Body Check, bringing your left elbow into contact with the base of your opponent's throat.

⑦⑧⑨⑩ Placing your weight heavily on your left foot, slide forward on your left foot, turning your elbow so that your forearm comes up, forcing your opponent to bend backward. Slide forward once again on your left foot to knock your opponent over, keeping your weight firmly on your front foot.

①

②

③

④

HIJI-SHIME 肘締め
Elbow Lock

SHOMEN UCHI HIJI-SHIME 1　正面打ち肘締め 1
Strike to the Forehead; Elbow Lock Type 1

① You and your opponent stand facing each other, right foot forward.

② Strike at your opponent's forehead with the side of your right hand. As your opponent blocks your blow, push his arm upward lifting him off balance.

③ Slide forward and cut downward with your hands in a similar way to that in the Strike to the Forehead; First Control Type 1 Throw, but do not cut down so far.

④ Sliding forward on your left foot, slide your left hand from your opponent's elbow along his forearm to grasp his wrist from underneath, trapping your opponent's arm under your left arm. Do not pull your opponent's arm into you, but rather push your chest forward to meet his arm.

⑤⑥ Pivoting on your left foot, rotate your right leg around anti-clockwise in a big circle. At the same time fold your right hand over your opponent's wrist from underneath. Focus the push generated from your hips into your left elbow to push diagonally downward, locking your opponent's elbow joint. Keep your weight firmly over your front (left) foot.

⑦⑧⑨ Enlarged photos of how to trap your opponent's elbow.

IMPORTANT POINTS

- When applying the elbow lock, drop your shoulder and stiffen the muscles in your waist and lower back.

①

②

③

④

⑤

⑥

⑦

⑧

⑨

Strike to the Forehead; Elbow Lock Type 2

① Stand facing your opponent in the basic stance, left foot forward. Your opponent stands right foot forward.

② Your opponent strikes at your forehead with the side of his right hand. Meet your opponent's strike by blocking with the side of your right wrist, and catching his elbow with your left hand.

③④ Pivoting on your left foot, and rotating your right foot clockwise around behind you, cut down in a spiral, letting your opponent's momentum carry him forward, in a way similar to that in the Strike to the Forehead; First Control Type 2 Throw. Trap your opponent's arm in the same way as in Elbow Lock Type 1.

⑤ Pivoting again on your left foot, rotate your right foot around anti-clockwise in a big circle, locking your opponent's elbow in the same way as in Elbow Lock Type 1.

IMPORTANT POINTS

- When trapping your opponent's elbow under your left arm, do not let your weight fall onto your back foot.

- Do not try to use just your arm strength to lock your opponent's elbow. Use the power generated by rotating your hips and right leg and shifting your body weight. Do not forget your posture.

①

②

③

④

⑤

KATA-MOCHI HIJI-SHIME 1 　肩持ち肘締め 1
Shoulder Grasp; Elbow Lock Type 1

① You and your opponent stand facing each other, right foot forward. Your opponent grasps your shirt in front of your left shoulder with his right hand and pulls.

② Using your opponent's pull, slide your back (left) foot diagonally to the left in a curve. At the same time, aim a back-handed punch to your opponent's face with your right hand, and thrust your left hand out, palm down, diagonally to your left in a curve.

③④ With your right hand, fix your opponent's right hand to your shoulder. Sliding forward on your front (right) foot, slide your opponent's elbow upward with your left wrist, forcing him off balance.

⑤ Sliding forward once more on your front (right) foot, cut down with the side of your left hand in a curve, turning your opponent's elbow over.

⑥ Take a large sliding step forward with your back (left) foot, fully stretching out your opponent's right arm, straightening his elbow, and trapping it between your chest and your left elbow.

⑦ Without relaxing your hold on your opponent's wrist and elbow, pivot on your front (left) foot, rotating your right leg around anti-clockwise. Use the force created by your rotation to lock out your opponent's elbow joint.

①

②

③

④

⑤

⑥

⑦

KATA-MOCHI HIJI-SHIME 2　肩持ち肘締め 2
Shoulder Grasp; Elbow Lock Type 2

① Stand facing your opponent, left foot forward. Your opponent stands right foot forward, grasps your shirt in front of your left shoulder, and pushes.

② Using your opponent's push, slide to your left on your front foot, aim a backhanded punch to your opponent's face with your right hand, and thrust your left hand out diagonally downward to your left in a circular motion. Slide your back foot up quickly in line with your left foot as your hips move forward.

③④ Grasp your opponent's right wrist with your right hand, fixing it to your shoulder. Bring your left wrist up to make contact with the elbow joint of your opponent's right arm.

Pivoting on your left foot, rotate your right leg clockwise 45 degrees, and thrust your opponent's elbow upward with the side of your left hand, forcing him off balance.

⑤⑥ Bring the side of your left hand round to the front, against your opponent's elbow. Pivoting once more on your left foot, rotate your right leg around behind you clockwise in a wide circle, and cut downward on your opponent's arm in a spiraling motion, forcing your opponent off balance.

⑦ Trap your opponent's elbow between your chest and your left elbow. Pivot on your left foot, this time rotating your right leg anti-clockwise to lock out your opponent's elbow joint.

①

②

③

④

⑤

⑥

⑦

Elbow Lock Timing Throw

In The Elbow Lock Timing Throws you make contact with your opponent's elbow with your arm, and by turning your arm over, lock out his elbow joint and throw him.

KATATE-MOCHI HIJI-ATE KOKYU-NAGE 1　片手持ち肘当て呼吸投げ 1
Wrist Grasp; Elbow Lock Timing Throw Type 1

In this throw, when your opponent grasps your wrist and pulls, you place your arm against his elbow, and time turning your hand over with a slide forward to lock his elbow joint and throw him.

① You and your opponent stand facing each other, right foot forward. Your opponent grasps your left wrist with his right hand and pulls.

② Using your opponent's pull, slide diagonally forward to your right, turning your hand over slightly.

③ At the same time as you slide your right foot forward, grasp your opponent's wrist with your right hand, free your left hand from his grasp, and place the inside of your left arm against your opponent's right elbow.

④ Slide forward on your left foot, and turn your hand palm down, thrusting your left arm out to lock out your opponent's elbow and throw him forward.

IMPORTANT POINTS

▪ Try not to lift your opponent's arm.

①

②

③

④

⑤

KATATE-MOCHI HIJI-ATE KOKYU-NAGE 2　片手持ち肘当て呼吸投げ 2

Wrist Grasp; Elbow Lock Timing Throw Type 2

① Stand facing your opponent in the basic stance, left foot forward. Your opponent stands right foot forward and grasps your left wrist with his right hand and pushes.

② Using your opponent's push and turning your hand palm down, pivot on your left foot, rotating your right foot around clockwise behind you.

③ While you are spinning around, grasp your opponent's right wrist with your right hand, free your left hand from his grasp, and immediately bring your left arm into contact with his right elbow.

④ Throw your opponent as per the Elbow Lock Timing Throw Type 1.

①

②

③

④

SUWARI WAZA YOKOMEN UCHI HIJI-ATE KOKYU-NAGE 1

座り技横面打ち肘当て呼吸投げ 1

Kneeling Strike to the Side of the Head; Elbow Lock Timing Throw Type 1

① You and your opponent kneel facing each other.

② Your opponent strikes at the side of your head with the side of his right hand. Sliding diagonally to your left, block the strike with your left wrist, and aim a backhanded punch to his face with your right hand.

③ Place your right wrist over your left forearm, trapping your opponent's right wrist in a cross.

④ Slide your right hand back to the right. (In the case of the First Control Throws, you cut downward in a curve with your wrist, but in the Elbow Lock Timing Throws you attempt rather to stretch out your opponent's arm.) Bring your left arm up under your opponent's elbow, with the fingers of your left

hand firmly spread, palm up, and your arm pointing forward and slightly down. Do not grasp your opponent's wrist with your right hand, but have your right arm pointing forward and slightly down (as thought you are sandwiching your opponent's elbow between your two arms).

⑤⑥ Push forward with your left knee and hip, quickly turning your left elbow and hand palm down, snapping your opponent's elbow straight, locking it, and throwing him forward.

IMPORTANT POINTS

- When you straighten your arm with a snap, make sure your left hand does not lag behind.

①

②

③

④

⑤ ⑥

As two opponents each go to grasp a knee, Gozo Shioda brings his knees together so that they lose their balance and crash into each other.

YOKOMEN UCHI HIJI-ATE KOKYU-NAGE 1　横面打ち肘当て呼吸投げ1
Strike to the Side of the Head; Elbow Lock Timing Throw Type 1

① You and your opponent stand facing each other, right foot forward.

② Your opponent strikes at the side of your head with the side of his right hand. Sliding diagonally to your left, block the strike with your left wrist, and aim a backhanded punch to his face with your right hand, so that your opponent is forced off balance.

③ Trap your opponent's wrist in a cross and, turning your hips to the right, slide your opponent's arm out in front of you, straightening out his elbow with your left arm under his elbow and your right wrist placed over his wrist. Place your weight over your right foot, and lower your center of balance.

④ Thrusting forward with your hips and your left foot, lock your opponent's elbow straight and throw him forward.

IMPORTANT POINTS

- Make sure your back (right) leg is straight. Especially when you try to lock your opponent's elbow, if your back knee is bent, you will be unable to use the strength from your hips and waist.

①

②

③

④

SHOMEN TSUKI HIJI-ATE KOKYU-NAGE 1　正面突き肘当て呼吸投げ 1
Punch to the Chest; Elbow Lock Timing Throw Type 1

① You and your opponent stand facing each other, right foot forward. As your opponent steps back with his right foot and prepares to punch you in the chest, take one sliding step forward on your front (right) foot to keep the distance between you the same.

②③ In timing with your opponent's punch, pivot on your back foot, rotating your right foot around three-quarters of the way behind you clockwise, and deflect your opponent's fist, letting his momentum carry him forward.

④⑤ Bring your left arm up against your opponent's right elbow, your palm up and elbow bent. With your right hand, lightly cover your opponent's right wrist.

⑤⑥ Slide forward on your front (left) foot, turning your left arm over, palm down as you do so, to lock your opponent's elbow and throw him forward. Keep your weight on your front foot.

①

②

③

④

⑤

⑥

SHOMEN TSUKI HIJI-ATE KOKYU-NAGE 2 　正面突き肘当て呼吸投げ 2
Punch to the Chest; Elbow Lock Timing Throw Type 2

①② Stand facing your opponent in the basic stance, left foot forward. Your opponent stands right foot forward. When he steps back with his right foot and prepares to punch you in the chest, take one sliding step forward on your front (left) foot.

③④⑤ In timing with your opponent's punch, pivot on your front (left) foot, rotating your back (right) leg around behind you clockwise. Deflect your opponent's punch with your left wrist, and bring your left arm up under his elbow joint, making a cross out of your left arm and his right arm. With your right hand, lightly cover your opponent's right wrist. Slide forward on your front (left) foot, turning your left arm over, palm down, to throw your opponent forward. Keep your weight on your front foot.

①

②

③

④

⑤

KOTE-GAESHI 小手返し
Wrist Throw

In the Wrist Throw, you bend your opponent's hand to the outside to lock his wrist joint and throw him.

SHOMEN UCHI KOTE-GAESHI 1   正面打ち小手返し 1
Strike to the Forehead; Wrist Throw Type 1

In this throw you get your opponent to stick out his arm by striking at his head, forcing him to block. You then twist his wrist to the outside to throw him.

① You and your opponent stand facing each other, right foot forward.

② Strike at your opponent's forehead with the side of your right hand, getting him to block your blow with his right forearm.

③ Pivot on your left foot. As you rotate your right foot clockwise and turn to face the opposite direction, grasp your opponent's hand with your left hand, and slide forward with your left foot, stretching your opponent's arm.

④ Turn back to face your opponent.

⑤ Placing your weight on your left foot as you turn around, bring your left hand over so that your opponent's wrist is bent to the outside. At the same time aim a backhanded punch to his face with your right hand.

⑥ Slide forward on your right foot, locking out your opponent's wrist, and throwing him.

⑦ Seize your opponent's elbow with your right hand, and turn him over, face down.

⑧ Press down on your opponent's shoulder, elbow, and wrist to finish.

⑨ How to lock the wrist: When throwing your opponent do not grip with your right hand, but place your hand over the back of his hand, and cut downward in the direction of his fingers.

⑩ How to grasp your opponent's hand: Place your thumb of your left hand between the knuckles of your opponent's little finger and ring finger, and grasp your opponent's palm below his thumb with your fingers. Bend his hand back to the outside.

①

②

③

④

⑤

⑥

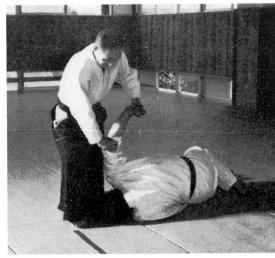

⑦

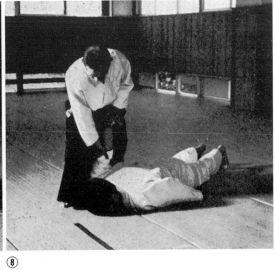

⑧

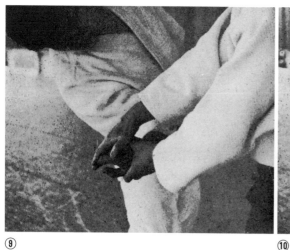

⑨

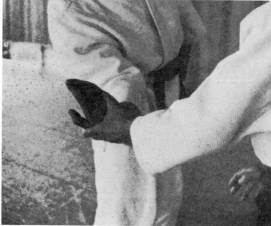

⑩

SHOMEN UCHI KOTE-GAESHI 2　正面打ち小手返し 2
Strike to the Forehead; Wrist Throw Type 2

① Stand facing your opponent in the basic stance, left foot forward. Your opponent stands right foot forward.

② When your opponent strikes at your forehead, block his blow with your right wrist, and meet his right elbow with your left hand.

③④ Using your opponent's push, pivot on your left foot, rotating your right foot around clockwise to 45 degrees diagonally behind your opponent. Allow your opponent's momentum to carry him forward bringing his right wrist down in a spiraling motion. Turn your hips to the right, transferring your weight from your left foot to your right foot, so that you face away from your opponent and, sliding your left hand down from your opponent's elbow to his wrist, grasp the back of his hand. Stretch your right hand out in front of you at chest height, as though in preparation for Body Line Exercise 2. All the above movements should be carried out in one fluid motion.

⑤⑥ Pivot on your front (right) foot, rotating your back (left) foot around behind you anti-clockwise more than 180 degrees.

At the same time, turn your opponent's hand over with your left hand, and aim a backhanded punch to his face with your right hand.

⑦⑧⑨ After punching at your opponent's face, with your right hand cover the back of his right hand, and pivot once more on your right foot, rotating your left foot in the same direction as before. At the same time, cut down strongly on your opponent's hand in the direction of his fingertips to throw him.

⑩⑪⑫ Slide your right hand from the back of your opponent's right hand to his right elbow, trapping it between your thumb and forefinger. Leading with your back foot, slide alongside your opponent's body, and at the same time turn his elbow around in the direction of his head, forcing him flat onto his stomach. Change your grip on your opponent's elbow with your right hand, so that your fingers are now pointing downward. Placing your weight heavily on your front (right) foot, press down and lock your opponent's wrist, elbow and shoulder joints to finish.

①

②

⑪

⑫

YOKOMEN UCHI KOTE-GAESHI 1　横面打ち小手返し 1
Strike to the Side of the Head; Wrist Throw Type 1

① You and your opponent stand facing each other, right foot forward.

②③ Your opponent strikes at the side of your head with the side of his right hand, and as in the Strike to the Side of the Head; Side Body Check Type 1 Throw, move your body to the left, block the blow, and unbalance your opponent.

④ Pivoting on your back (left) foot, rotate your right foot around clockwise diagonally behind you, grasp your opponent's hand with your left hand, and stretch your right arm out in front of you, remaining aware of all that is going on around you. Transfer your weight from your left foot to your right foot quickly, as you turn your hips to the right. Slide forward, lowering your center of gravity to pull your opponent off balance and cause him to fall forward. For the remaining moves of this throw, also refer to the explanation for the Strike to the Forehead; Wrist Throw Type 1 Throw.

④'④"④'" Photos ④', ④", and ④'" show the steps in point ④ of deflecting your opponent's hand, grasping his hand, and stretching him off balance.

⑤ Turn back to face your opponent, putting your weight back onto your left foot, bending his hand over and to the outside with your left hand, and aim a backhanded punch to his face with your right hand. When bending your opponent's hand over, do it in a small, quick, circular motion. Maintain the pressure on your opponent's hand to prevent him from standing up straight and recovering his balance.

⑥ Sliding forward on your right foot, cover the back of your opponent's hand with your right hand and cut downward, throwing him. Do not grasp your opponent's hand with your right hand.

⑦⑧ Grasp your opponent's elbow with your right hand (so that your thumb is closest to you). Turn your opponent's elbow around in a winding movement, and bring your left foot close into his body as he is forced to roll over, face down.

⑨ Change your grip on your opponent's elbow with your right hand (so that the thumb side of your hand is down), and press down on his elbow and wrist.

①

②

③

④'

④"

④

④'''

⑤

⑥

⑦

⑧

⑨

RYOTE-MOCHI KOTE-GAESHI 両手持ち小手返し
Double Wrist Grasp; Wrist Throw

The way of grasping and bending your opponent's wrist:

The method of turning your opponent's wrist to the outside and bending it backward from a double wrist grasp differs from the techniques used for the throws that start from a Strike to the Forehead or a Punch to the Chest. It is, therefore, necessary to learn both methods.

① Your opponent grasps both your wrists.

② Turn your hands over palm up, and press the back of your right hand to your left palm. With your left hand, hook your little finger, ring finger, and middle finger around the base of your opponent's thumb, holding his hand in place, and trapping your opponent's wrist between your thumb and index finger (similar to the grasp used for the Third Control). Keep the palm of your right hand facing up.

③ Thrust the thumb side of your left hand forward, keeping your little finger fixed (do not twist), and with your right hand bend your wrist below your little finger against your opponent's thumb and push forward to release your right hand. Do not simply try to force your hand upward to remove your hand from your opponent's grasp.

④ Bend your opponent's wrist back to the outside, place your right hand over the back of your opponent's left hand, and cut down with the side of your hand to throw your opponent.

IMPORTANT POINTS

- It is easier to remove your hand from your opponent's grip if you do not pull your hands in toward you, but push your hands forward.

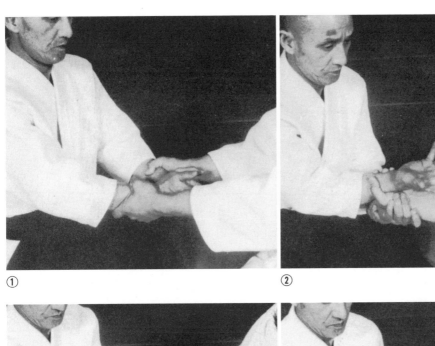

①   ②

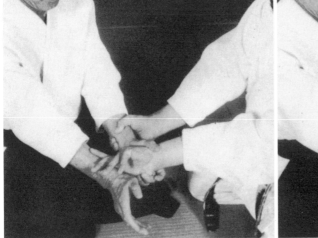
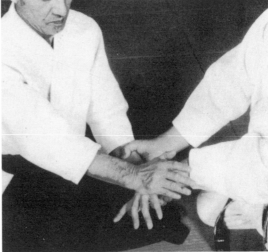

③   ④

SUWARI WAZA RYOTE-MOCHI KOTE-GAESHI 1　座り技両手持ち小手返し 1
Kneeling Double Wrist Grasp; Wrist Throw Type 1

① You and your opponent kneel opposite each other. Your opponent grasps both your wrists and pulls.

② Using your opponent's pull, slide diagonally forward to the right on your right knee. Follow the instructions for point 2 of the above Double Wrist Grasp; Wrist Throw explanation.

③ Slide forward on your right knee and remove your right hand from your opponent's grip.

④ Quickly cover the back of your opponent's left hand with the side of your right hand.

⑤ Sliding forward on your left knee, cut down on your opponent's wrist, bending it backward and throwing him.

IMPORTANT POINTS

- The finishing arm lock is the same as the technique used for the Second Control arm lock (pin).

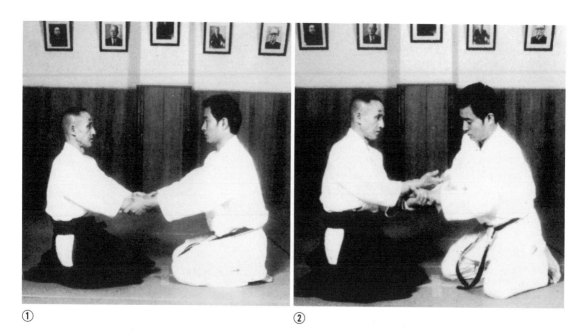

①

②

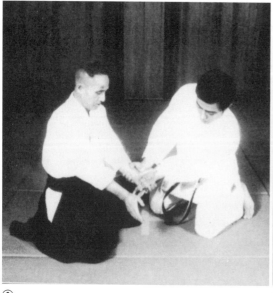

③

④

⑤

SUWARI WAZA RYOTE-MOCHI KOTE-GAESHI 2　座り技両手持ち小手返し 2
Kneeling Double Wrist Grasp; Wrist Throw Type 2

① You and your opponent kneel facing each other. Your opponent grasps both your wrists and pushes.

② Using your opponent's push, pivot on your left knee, rotating your right knee around behind you clockwise. Turn your hands over and grasp your opponent's left hand in the same way as in the Kneeling Double Wrist Grasp; Wrist Throw Type 1.

③ Rotating your right knee around behind you clockwise once more, cut down on your opponent's hand bending his wrist backward and throwing him out in front of you.

④ Having thrown your opponent, cover your opponent's wrist with your right hand, and bring the side of your left hand up against his elbow joint. Bend your opponent's wrist, elbow, and shoulder joints up over his head in a circular motion, and apply the finishing arm lock using the same technique as in the Second Control arm lock (pin).

①

②

③

④

Punch to the Chest; Wrist Throw Type 1

① You and your opponent stand facing each other, right foot forward. Your opponent steps back with his right foot and prepares to punch you in the chest. As he does so, take one sliding step forward on your front (right) foot.

②③④ In timing with your opponent's punch, rotate your right foot around clockwise behind you diagonally to your left, and turn your hips clockwise to face away from your opponent. As you do so, slide your left hand down to your opponent's fist and transfer your weight to your right foot, unbalancing your opponent by assuming a similar posture as in Body Line Exercise Type 2.

⑤ Transfer your weight back onto your left foot from your right foot, and turn to face your opponent. Slide diagonally forward to your left on your left foot and bend your opponent's hand back to the outside with your left hand. With your right hand, aim a backhanded punch to your opponent's face.

⑥⑦⑧ Place the palm of your right hand over the back of your opponent's right hand. Take a large sliding step forward with your back (right) foot, cutting down with your right hand in the direction of your opponent's right hand's fingers to throw him. Grasp your opponent's right elbow with your right hand, trapping his elbow between your thumb and forefinger, and turn his elbow around in a winding movement so that he is forced to roll over onto his face, and bring your left foot around alongside his body. Change your right hand's grip and, putting your weight firmly on your front (right) foot, push down, locking your opponent's wrist, elbow, and shoulder joints.

①

②

③

④

⑤

⑥

⑦

⑧

▌ SHOMEN TSUKI KOTE-GAESHI 2　正面突き小手返し 2
▌ Punch to the Chest; Wrist Throw Type 2

① Stand facing your opponent, left foot forward. Your opponent stands right foot forward. When he steps back with his right foot and prepares to punch you in the chest, take one sliding step forward on your front (left) foot.

②③ In timing with your opponent's punch, pivot on your front (left) foot, rotating your back (right) leg around behind you clockwise 120 degrees. Slide your left hand down to grasp your opponent's right fist, and turn to face away from your opponent, transferring your weight to your right foot, unbalancing your opponent by assuming a similar posture as in Body Line Exercise Type 2.

④⑤⑥ Pivot on your right foot, rotating your back (left) foot around anticlockwise behind you more than 180 degrees, so that you face your opponent. With your left hand, bend your opponent's right wrist back and to the outside, and with your right hand, aim a backhanded punch to his face. Rotate your left foot around anticlockwise once more, covering the back of your opponent's right hand with your right palm, and throw him by bending his wrist backward.

⑦⑧ Roll your opponent over onto his stomach as you move alongside him. Finally, lock out his wrist, elbow, and shoulder joints by pushing down.

The Timing Throws are practiced in order to develop your ability to focus your strength and to raise your understanding of your opponent's intentions, both of which are necessary for performing all Aikido techniques. Here we shall focus on throws used where you are pulled or pushed, but in reality there are a great number of different timing throws for different situations.

SUWARI RYOTE-MOCHI KOKYU-HO 1　座り両手持ち呼吸法 1
Kneeling Double Wrist Grasp; Timing Throw Type 1

① You and your opponent stand facing each other in the basic stance, right foot forward, before kneeling.

② Your opponent grasps both your wrists from the outer side and pulls.

③ Using your opponent's pull and keeping your hands, feet, and hips all in line, swing your hands up in a circular motion, as though raising a sword. At the same time, bring the toes of both feet up under you.

④ Slide to your left on your left knee, unbalancing your opponent, without pulling or bending your arms (especially your left arm). With the sides of your hands, cut down diagonally forward to the left. As your opponent falls backward, slide with him on your knees. As you slide forward on your knees, keep your hips pushed forward to apply even pressure to your left and right hands.

⑤ Straighten your posture as you exhale, while your opponent lies flat on his back. Do not lean or bend over your opponent.

③" This photo shows point 3 from the rear. Hands, feet, and hips are all in line, and the shoulders are down.

④" This photo shows point 4 from the rear. Move to the side, keeping your hands up in the same posture.

②'③'④' These photos show a close up of the hands for points ②, ③, and ④, and how to raise your hands.

IMPORTANT POINTS

- In point ③, do not try to lift your opponent up. Keep your arms in tight.

①

②

②'

③

③'

③"

④

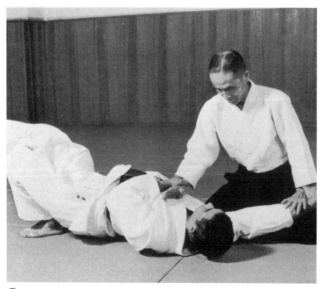

④′

④″

⑤

SUWARI RYOTE-MOCHI KOKYU-HO 2　座り両手持ち呼吸法 2

Kneeling Double Wrist Grasp; Timing Throw Type 2

① You and your opponent kneel facing each other. Your opponent grasps both your wrists and pushes.

② Using your opponent's push, slide your wrists and fingers over the inside of your opponent's wrist in a circular movement as your turn your hands upward, and raise your hands, to adopt the same posture as in the Kneeling Double Wrist Grasp; Timing Throw Type 1.

③ Slide to the left on your left knee, and follow the same instructions as for the Kneeling Double Wrist Grasp; Timing Throw Type 1.

④ Straighten out your posture.

②'③' These photos show points ② and ③ from the rear. The spacing of the hands is wider than for the Kneeling Double Wrist Grasp; Timing Throw Type 1.

⑤⑥⑦ These photos show how to raise your hands.

IMPORTANT POINTS

- In point ②, do not pull. Keep your elbows and shoulders down.

①

② ②'

③

③′

④

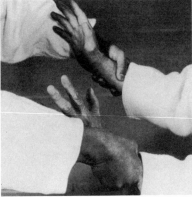

⑤

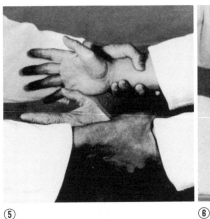

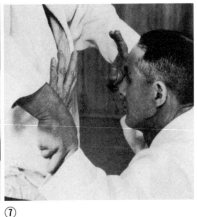

⑥

⑦

SUWARI RYOTE-MOCHI KOKYU-HO 3 　座り両手持ち呼吸法 3
Kneeling Double Wrist Grasp; Timing Throw Type 3

① You and your opponent kneel facing each other.

② Your opponent grasps both your wrists from the outside and holds them in place.

③ Bringing your toes up under your feet and keeping your hips down, turn your hands palm up, to place the backs of your hands on the inside of your opponent's wrists. Put your weight into your wrists and hands.

④ Pushing your hips forward, thrust your hands, fingers open stiffly, in the direction of your opponent's elbows, until his arms are bent under him, rendering him powerless.

⑤ In the same way as in the Kneeling Double Wrist Grasp; Timing Throw Type 1, raise your hands up in a circular motion, lifting your opponent up and off balance.

⑥⑦ In the same way as in the Kneeling Double Wrist Grasp; Timing Throw Type 1, keep your hands in the same position as you slide to the left on your left knee, unbalancing your opponent.

⑧⑨⑩ Cut down with the sides of both hands diagonally to your left, and as your opponent falls backward, slide forward with him under your control, as in the Kneeling Double Wrist Grasp; Timing Throw Type 1.

IMPORTANT POINTS

- In point ③, when you turn your hands over, move your hands in a circular motion. Do not pull. If you try to place your hands straight on the inside of your opponent's wrists, you will be likely to lift your shoulders, making it difficult to put your weight into your hands.

- In point ⑤, do not try to lift your opponent up. Keep your shoulders down. Keep your hands, feet, and hips in a line.

- In point ⑦, when you cut down, do not use your arm strength to push your opponent down, but use the thrust from your hips.

①

②

③

④

⑤

⑥

⑦

⑧

⑨

⑩

SUWARI RYOTE-MOCHI KOKYU-HO 4 　座り両手持ち呼吸法 4

Kneeling Double Wrist Grasp; Timing Throw Type 4

① You and your opponent kneel facing each other. Your opponent grasps both your wrists from underneath and holds them fixed, stopping you from pulling your elbows in.

②③ Bring your hands together in front of you, placing the back of your right hand over the palm of your left hand, and with your left hand against your opponent's left wrist. Turning your left hand palm down, slide your left hand along your opponent's forearm toward his elbow, leading with your little finger, closing your hand into a fist as you do. Close your right hand into a fist, too.

④ Slide forward on your right knee. Use the strength from your hips to lean forward with your upper body, forcing your opponent off balance. Thrust your right fist toward your opponent's face. After sliding forward, bring your toes up under your feet.

①

②

③

④

SUWARI RYOTE-MOCHI KOKYU-HO 5 座り両手持ち呼吸法 5

Kneeling Double Wrist Grasp; Timing Throw Type 5

① You and your opponent kneel facing each other.

②③ Place your hands flat on your knees. Your opponent grasps both your wrists and fixes your hands against your knees.

④⑤ Pivoting on your right knee, slide your left knee around behind you. In the same way as in the Wrist Grasp; Multi-Directional Throws, turn your right hand to the inside in a circular motion with your palm down, and when your opponent's left arm is stretched out and your opponent off balance, turn your palm up and cut downward along your opponent's right arm from his elbow to his wrist. At the same time, turn your

left hand, still flat on your knee, around in a circular motion to the outside, leading with your little finger, causing your opponent to fall off balance diagonally to your left.

⑥⑦ Rotating your left knee around behind you once more, turn your right wrist over and cut downward with the side of your hand to throw your opponent.

IMPORTANT POINTS

- All the Timing Throws are techniques to enable you to develop strength through timing, essential for mastering all Aikido techniques.

①

②

③

RYOTE-MOCHI TENCHI NAGE 両手持ち天地投げ
Double Wrist Grasp; Heaven and Earth Throw

In the Heaven and Earth Throws you spread your arms, holding one hand up and the other down, in other words stretching one hand to Heaven and the other toward the Earth, to unbalance and throw your opponent.

SUWARI RYOTE-MOCHI TENCHI NAGE 1 座り両手持ち天地投げ 1
Kneeling Double Wrist Grasp; Heaven and Earth Throw Type 1

In this throw, when your opponent grasps both your wrists and pulls, you respond by moving your hands in different directions and with unequal strength.

① You and your opponent stand facing each other in the basic stance, right foot forward, before kneeling.

② Your opponent grasps both your wrists and pulls.

③ Using your opponent's pull, swing your right hand up, and slide your left hand down and around behind your opponent. At the same time, slide forward diagonally to the left on your left knee.

④ Cut forward with your hands as though to bring them together behind your opponent's back. At the same time slide diagonally forward to the right on your right knee, throwing your opponent on his back.

IMPORTANT POINTS

- Your right hand should be on the inside of your opponent's wrist. Your left hand should be on the outside.
- When throwing your opponent, do not get on top of him.

①

②

③

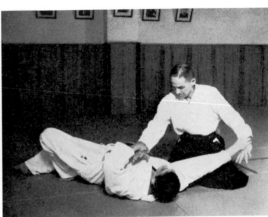

④

RYOTE-MOCHI TENCHI NAGE 1 　両手持ち天地投げ 1
Double Wrist Grasp; Heaven and Earth Throw Type 1

① You and your opponent stand facing each other, right foot forward.

② Your opponent grasps both your wrists and pulls.

③ Using your opponent's pull, swing your right hand up, and slide your left hand down and around behind your opponent. At the same time, slide forward diagonally to the left and around behind your opponent in a circular movement on your left foot.

④⑤ Cut forward with your hands as though to bring them together behind your opponent's back. At the same time slide diagonally forward to the right on your right foot, throwing your opponent on his back.

①

②

③

④

⑤

SUWARI RYOTE-MOCHI TENCHI NAGE 2 　座り両手持ち天地投げ2

Kneeling Double Wrist Grasp; Heaven and Earth Throw Type 2

① You and your opponent kneel opposite each other. Your opponent grasps both your wrists and pushes.

②③ Using your opponent's push, pivot on your left knee, rotating your right knee around clockwise behind you. Bring your right hand up in a circular movement on the inside of your opponent's wrist, and turn your left hand over with the palm facing upward to unbalance your opponent.

④ Slide diagonally forward to the left on your left knee. Turning your left hand over, palm down, slide it around behind your opponent in a circular movement. Bring your right hand

up in the direction of your opponent's left shoulder, so that his elbow is forced upward, and he is brought further off balance.

⑤ Slide diagonally behind your opponent on your right knee, turning your right hand over so that your thumb is facing down, and thrust your right hand forward from your opponent's shoulder toward his back. At the same time, thrust your left hand out in the direction of your thumb in a circular movement, throwing your opponent on his back. Keep your body weight leaning forward.

①

②

③

④

⑤

RYOTE-MOCHI TENCHI NAGE 2　両手持ち天地投げ 2
Double Wrist Grasp; Heaven and Earth Throw Type 2

① Stand facing your opponent, left foot forward. Your opponent stands right foot forward, grasps both your wrists, and pushes.

②③ In the same way as in Finishing Exercise Type 2, pivot on your left foot, rotating your right leg clockwise around behind you. Raise your right hand up on the inside of your opponent's left wrist. Your left hand swings around in front of you, palm up. Sliding diagonally forward to the left on your left foot, turn your left hand over, palm down, sliding it around behind your opponent in a circular movement. Bring

your right hand up in the direction of your opponent's left shoulder, so that his elbow is forced upward, and he is brought further off balance. Your right foot should mirror the movement of your left foot, and slide around diagonally to the left.

④⑤ Slide diagonally to the right behind your opponent on your right foot. At the same time push your left hand forward and, turning your right hand over so that your thumb is facing down, thrust your right hand around behind your opponent, throwing him on his back. Keep your body weight leaning forward.

①

②

③

④

⑤

CHAPTER 3
PRACTICAL APPLICATION THROWS 応用技法

KATA-MOCHI IKKAJO-NAGE　肩持ち一ヵ条投げ
Shoulder Grasp; First Control Throw

① Stand facing your opponent, left foot forward. Your opponent stands right foot forward. For all of these practical application throws, the spacing between you and your opponent is wider than normal spacing, as the moves start with your opponent rushing toward you.

② Your opponent rushes toward you and attempts to grasp your shirt in front of your left shoulder with his right hand.

③ Without looking directly at the hand coming at your shoulder, and timing your move with your opponent's approach, cover the back of your opponent's right hand with your right hand from above.

④ As you cover your opponent's hand, pivot on your back (right) foot, rotating your left foot around anti-clockwise behind you, letting your opponent's momentum carry him forward and off balance.

⑤ Slide forward on your right foot, placing your weight on your right foot, and bringing the side of your left hand up against your opponent's right elbow. Make sure that your left hand is in line with your feet and hips, directly in front of you.

⑥ Slide forward on your left foot, pushing forward with your hips, lowering your center of balance, and at the same time cut down and push forward with both hands, bringing them to your chest level.

⑦ Having thrown your opponent, remain in this position, with your weight firmly on your front foot.

①

②

③

④

⑤

⑥

⑦

SHOMEN UCHI USHIRO-NAGE　正面打ち後ろ投げ
Strike to the Forehead; Throw from Behind

① Stand facing your opponent in the basic stance, left foot forward. Your opponent stands right foot forward.

② As your opponent goes to strike at your forehead with the side of his right hand, slide diagonally forward to your left.

③ As your opponent misses you and his momentum carries him past you, come around behind him.

④ With your left foot forward, place your hands on your opponent's shoulders. Do not grip.

⑤ Slide backward in the same way as in Body Line Exercise 1, moving your feet and hips backward together, and pulling your opponent over backward.

①

②

③

④

⑤

YOKOMEN UCHI SHIHO-NAGE KUZUSHI　横面打ち四方投げ崩し

Strike to the Side of the Head; Abridged Multi-Directional Throw

① You and your opponent stand facing each other, right foot forward.

② As your opponent raises his hands, preparing to strike at the side of your head, raise your own hands over your head, preparing to block his attack.

③ Your opponent advances and strikes at your left temple with the side of his right hand. Deflect your opponent's right hand to the outside with your left hand as you pivot on your right foot, rotating your left foot around anti-clockwise behind you.

④ Rotate your left foot around 120 degrees, cutting diagonally downward with your left hand to your chest level, looking your opponent in the eyes all the time.

⑤ Point 4 seen from a different angle.

⑥ As in the standard Multi-Directional Throws, slide diagonally forward on your right foot, bringing your opponent's right hand to a point directly in front of you, in line with your feet and hips.

⑦ Slide your left foot forward, bringing your opponent's hand up over your head. At this time do not put your weight on your left foot.

⑧ Turn around to your right, putting your weight on your right foot.

⑨ Bring your opponent's hand down in front of your face, making sure you keep your weight firmly on your right foot.

⑩ As in Body Line Exercise Type 1, slide your feet and hips forward, and at the same time throw forward with your right hand. The difference with the standard Multi-Directional Throw is that your opponent's wrist is to the side, not directly over your hand.

⑪ Keep your weight on your front foot, and keep looking straight at your opponent.

①

②

③

④

⑤   ⑥

⑦

⑧

⑨

⑩

⑪

■ AYA-MOCHI SHOMEN IRIMI-NAGE 綾持ち正面入身投げ
Over-Wrist Grasp; Frontal Body Check

① You and your opponent stand facing each other, right foot forward. Look your opponent in the eye. Make sure that the spacing between you is sufficiently wide.

② Your opponent advances and goes to grasp your right wrist with his right hand, from above.

③ Pivot on your right foot, rotating your left foot around anti-clockwise over 120 degrees, allowing your opponent's momentum to carry him forward and leading him into an off-balance position.

④ Bring your right hand around in front of you, and raise it up high.

⑤ Rotating as in Body Movement Exercise Type 2, bring your right hand down in a spiral, spinning around clockwise to bring your opponent further off balance.

⑥ With your opponent off balance and falling forward, aim a punch to his face with your left hand.

⑦ As your opponent jerks backward to avoid your punch, transfer your weight from your right foot to your left foot, turning to face the opposite direction, as in Body Line Exercise Type 2. At the same time, slide the side of your right hand up from your opponent's chest to his throat.

⑧ Place your weight firmly on your left foot and push your right hand diagonally forward, to give you more stability.

⑨ Slide your back (right) foot forward, diagonally behind your opponent to throw him on his back. Having thrown your opponent, keep looking straight at him, and keep your weight on your front foot.

①

②

③

④

⑤

⑥

⑦

⑧

⑨

SHOMEN UCHI UDE-GARAMI-NAGE 正面打ち腕絡み投げ
Strike to the Forehead; Entwined Arm Throw

① Stand facing your opponent, left foot forward. Your opponent stands right foot forward, and advances to strike at your forehead with the side of his right hand.

②③ Block your opponent's blow, and allow his momentum to carry him past you on your right.

④ Keeping your opponent at arm's length, pivot on your left foot, rotating your right foot around clockwise in a large circle, bringing your opponent off balance.

⑤ With your opponent off balance, slide your left hand under the inside of your opponent's right forearm, and grasp your own right wrist.

⑥ Keeping your right forearm pressed tightly against your opponent's right elbow, entwine your opponent's right arm in your arms.

⑦⑧⑨ Keeping your opponent's arm tightly entwined, transfer your weight from your right foot to your left foot, turning to face the opposite direction, and bringing your right knee to the floor. Use the force generated from transferring your weight and cutting downward to throw your opponent out in front of you.

⑩⑪ Keeping your opponent's arm entwined, put your weight firmly on your left foot, and straighten your back to lock out your opponent's arm.

①

②

③

④

⑤　　　　　　　　　⑥　　　　　　　　　⑦

⑧　　　　　　　　　⑨　　　　　　　　　⑩

⑪

YOKOMEN UCHI KOSHI-NAGE　横面打ち腰投げ

Strike to the Side of the Head; Hip Throw

① You and your opponent stand facing each other, right foot forward. Your opponent prepares to strike at the side of your head.

②③ Your opponent advances, striking at your temple with the side of his right hand.

④ Pivot on your right foot, and deflect your opponent's blow so that he is brought off balance.

⑤ Keeping your weight on your right foot, bring your opponent's right arm around in front of you.

⑥⑦ Slide your left foot forward to a point between your opponent's feet, and transfer your weight onto your left foot.

⑧ Bring your opponent's body up onto your hip.

⑨⑩ By transferring your weight from your left foot to your right foot, your opponent will be lifted up and thrown.

①

②

③

④

⑤

⑥

⑦

⑧

⑨

⑩

SHOMEN YOKOMEN UCHI SHIHO-NAGE　正面・横面打ち四方投げ
Strike to the Forehead and Side of the Head; Multi-Directional Throw

① You and your opponent stand facing each other, right foot forward.

② When your opponent strikes at your forehead, push forward with your hips and block his blow strongly.

③④⑤ Your opponent cuts your right arm down, forcing you to your left. He then grasps the shirt in front of your left shoulder and, pivoting on his left foot, goes to strike at your left temple with the side of his right hand.

⑥ When your opponent strikes, pivot on your right foot, rotating your left leg around anti-clockwise, so that your opponent's momentum carries him past you. Aim a backhanded punch to his face with your right hand.

⑦ Sliding forward on your right foot, bring your opponent's outstretched right arm out in front of you.

⑧ Take a large sliding step forward on your left foot, and placing your weight firmly over your left foot, raise your hands up in front of your face.

⑨ Transfer your weight from your left foot to your right foot, turning your upper body around to the right to face the opposite direction, and unbalancing your opponent. Bend your opponent's arm over backward in front of you. Bring your hands down to your chest level.

⑩ Slide forward, moving your feet, hips, and right foot all at the same time, keeping your weight firmly on your right foot. Increasing the pressure on your opponent's wrist bent over his shoulder, throw your opponent down onto his back.

⑪⑫ Keeping your back straight, raise your right hand over your head and swing down hard with the side of your right hand, aiming for the spot between your opponent's eyebrows.

①

②

③

④

⑤

⑥

⑦

⑧

⑨

⑩

⑪

⑫

USHIRO RYOTE-MOCHI JUJI-NAGE　後ろ両手持ち十字投げ
Double Wrist Grasp from Behind; Crossed Arm Throw

① You and your opponent stand facing each other, right foot forward.

②③ Your opponent strikes at your forehead. Block the blow with the side of your right wrist, and aim a punch at your opponent's stomach with your left fist. Your opponent cuts your right hand down and then goes around you on your right-hand side. (See the explanation for Preparatory Exercise for Throws Where Your Opponent Attacks from Behind.)

④ Your opponent grasps both your wrists firmly. Lower your center of gravity in preparation for your opponent's pulling movement so that you are not pulled off balance.

⑤ Thrust out both hands in front of you, unbalancing your opponent. Then bring both hands up over your head in a large circle.

⑥⑦ Slide your right foot diagonally backward, placing your weight on your left foot, and cross your opponent's left arm over his right arm so that his elbows are touching.

⑧⑨ Sliding forward on your right foot, push forward, locking your opponent's elbow joints and throwing him out in front of you.

①

②

③

④

⑤

⑥

⑦

⑧

⑨

USHIRO RYOTE-MOCHI KOTE-GAESHI (OYO) 後ろ両手持ち小手返し（応用）
Double Wrist Grasp from Behind; Wrist Throw (Practical Application)

① You and your opponent stand facing each other, right foot forward.

②③④ Your opponent strikes at your forehead, and as he goes to move around behind you, pivot on your right foot, turning to your left, and rotating your left foot around anti-clockwise over 180 degrees, so that you and your opponent cross past each other.

⑤ Your opponent grasps your left wrist from the inside, with his left hand, palm up.

⑥⑦⑧ Slide your right hand down your opponent's left wrist to grasp the back of his left hand. Turn his hand over to the outside and lock out his wrist joint with the palm of your left hand. At the same time pivot on your left foot, rotating your right foot around clockwise in a large circle, moving your feet, hands, and hips all together to throw your opponent out in front of you.

①

②

③

④

⑤

⑥

⑦

⑧

AYA-MOCHI SOKUMEN IRIMI-NAGE 綾持ち側面入身投げ
Over-Wrist Grasp; Side Body Check

① You and your opponent stand facing each other, right foot forward.

② Your opponent advances and goes to grasp your right wrist from above with his right hand. As he does so, pivot on your right foot, rotating your back (left) foot around behind you in a large circle, allowing your opponent's momentum to carry him forward.

③ Raise your right hand up over your head, in line with your hips and feet.

④⑤ Turning to your right and under your right hand, slide your left foot forward, and as you place your weight on it,

rotate your right foot around clockwise behind you, bringing your right hand down in a spiraling motion.

⑥ Bring your left arm up, pressing tightly against your opponent's chest and throat, with your left hand palm up. Place the side of your right hand against your opponent's stomach. Put your weight firmly on your left foot.

⑦⑧ Slide forward, pushing with your legs, hips, and arms all in unison to throw your opponent onto his back. Keep looking straight at your opponent, and keep your weight on your front foot.

① ② ③

④ ⑤ ⑥

⑦ ⑧

KATATE AYA-MOCHI NIKAJO KARA NO UDE-GARAMI

片手綾持ち二ヵ条からの腕絡み

Over-Wrist Grasp; Entwined Arm Throw from the Second Control

①②③ You and your opponent stand facing each other, right foot forward. When your opponent advances and tries to grasp your right hand, pivot on your right foot, rotating your left leg around anti-clockwise 120 degrees. After spinning you should come to a stop in the Basic Stance, right foot forward.

④ Cover the back of your opponent's right hand with your left hand, fixing it to your right wrist.

⑤ Placing your weight on your right foot, cut down with your right hand, using the Second Control technique.

⑥ As your opponent starts to stand up again, transfer your weight from your right foot to your left foot and, fix his right elbow to your right elbow with your left hand, grasping his wrist with your right hand as you do so.

⑦ This photo shows how to hold your opponent's arm.

⑧⑨ As you transfer your body weight to your left foot, turn your hips to the left. Bringing your right knee to the floor, cut down and throw your opponent.

⑩ Keeping your back straight and your hold on your opponent's arm the same, place your weight strongly on your left foot. Maintaining your balance, force your opponent into submission.

③

②

①

④

⑤

⑥

⑦

⑧

⑨

⑩

KUBI SHIME KOKYU-NAGE　首締め呼吸投げ

Strangle Hold; Timing Throw

① You and your opponent stand facing each other, right foot forward.

② Your opponent grasps your collar with both hands, drawing your collar in tight on your throat.

③ Place your right hand on the inside of your opponent's left elbow, and push diagonally forward to bend his arm downward. At the same time, place your left hand on the side of your opponent's right elbow, pushing in the same direction as your right hand.

④ Slide diagonally forward to your right on your front (right) foot, bringing your left hand up and in line with your feet and

hips in front of you as you move. Push your right hand out diagonally forward to your right, forcing your opponent off balance. At this time, make sure your weight is firmly over your right foot, and that you maintain a stable posture.

⑤⑧ Slide your left foot forward, moving your hands, legs, and hips all at the same time to throw your opponent. Keep your weight on your front (left) foot after throwing your opponent.

①

②

③

④

⑤

⑥

FUTARI DORI RYOTE-MOCHI KOKYU-NAGE 二人取り両手持ち呼吸投げ
Two Opponents Double Wrist Grasp; Timing Throw

① Your two opponents stand diagonally in front of you, one on each side. They grasp your wrists with both hands, and push.

② Lower your center of gravity so that you are not pushed backward, and raise both hands so that your opponents' momentum carries them forward and up off balance.

③④⑤ Slide your right foot forward, lowering your center of balance as far as your can. Pushing strongly with your hips and, taking care to maintain your posture, throw your opponents forward with a big swing of your arms.

①

②

③

④

⑤

SEIZA-HO TO REI-HO　正座法と礼法
Formal Kneeling Method and Formal Bowing Method

The Formal Kneeling Method describes the correct way to kneel. By following the correct form and posture as you kneel, you will also learn to calm yourself. As such, it is an essential practice in Aikido, in which we attempt to achieve harmony between our emotions and our physical moves. The Formal Kneeling Method is also a basic technique used in throws that start from the kneeling position. When practicing these throws, it is essential to use the Formal Kneeling Method to kneel before performing the throw.

Bowing formally is an expression of humbleness. It represents our gratitude, and creates feelings of magnanimity. Bowing is the physical expression of having our emotions under control. In order to show our correct mood, a correct posture is vital. Here the Formal Bowing Method is shown as performed alone. When performed facing a partner, it is essential to perform it with the same timing and feeling as your partner.

① Stand in the Basic Stance, right foot forward.

② Keeping your hands outstretched in the Basic Stance, lower your hips straight down until your left knee reaches the floor just by the instep of your right foot.

③ Sliding your right leg back to kneel alongside your left knee, lay your hands lightly on your lap, with your fingers straight but not spread out. Keeping your toes bent up under

you, lower your hips onto your heels. Move your feet, hands, and hips all at the same time.

④ Keeping your hips on your heels, push with your toes so that your knees slide forward and your toes become straight. Your big toes should be together, side by side. Your feet should not overlap. The space between your knees should be a little less than one fist. Keep looking straight ahead.

⑤ Keeping your hips firmly on your heels, and your back and neck straight, lower your upper body, leaning forward, and slide your hands lightly past your knees and onto the floor with your fingers still straight and together. If you are kneeling opposite a partner, keep your focus on his eyes.

⑥ Bending your elbows, and bending further at the hips, lower your upper body. At this time make sure that your hips, back, and neck are all in a straight line.

⑦ Raise your upper body to assume the same position as in point 5.

⑧ Raise your upper body further, and slide your hands back onto your lap to achieve your original kneeling posture. When standing up, repeat the steps above in reverse to return to your original Basic Stance, right foot forward.

⑨⑩⑪ The photos show points ④, ⑤, and ⑧ from the front.

①

②

③

④ ⑤ ⑥ ⑦

⑧ ⑨ ⑩ ⑪

SHIKKO-HO 膝行法
Moving on your Knees

Moving on your knees involves moving forward, backward, to the side, and rotating whilst remaining in a kneeling position. It is important to retain your stability and balance as you perform this basic exercise. Mastery of these techniques is essential in order to perform the throws in Aikido that start from the kneeling position. Here the most basic form of moving on your knees, moving forward, is explained.

① Kneel (using the Formal Kneeling Method).

② With your hips firmly on your feet, bend your toes up underneath you, pushing your hips up with your heels. Keep looking straight ahead, and keep your hands flat on your lap near your groin. Do not tense the muscles in your upper body. From this posture, using your right knee as a fulcrum, slide your left knee forward. At the same time as you slide your left knee forward, slide your feet quickly to keep your heels together. Keep looking straight ahead.

③ Point ② seen from behind.

④ Use the above technique, sliding forward on your right knee and your left knee in turn to move forward.

① ② ③ ④

UKEMI 受け身
Falling Techniques

In practicing Aikido, we learn several different methods of falling safely when being thrown. These methods include the back fall, backward roll, forward roll, forward somersault, and backward somersault. Here the two most basic methods of falling—the back fall and the forward roll—are explained.

KOHO UKEMI 後方受け身
Back Fall

① From a standing position, bend both your knees. Lower your hips and stretch both arms out in front of you. Keep your fingers straight in preparation to slap the floor with both hands.

②③ Fall backward, rounding your body, bending your hips, waist, and back in that order. Stretch out both legs together in front of you. At the same time, making sure your arms are not bent at the elbows, slap the floor hard with both hands. Your hands should hit the floor just as your back makes contact with the floor.

Bend your back, bring your feet up, and use your abdominal muscles and swing from your arms to stand up and return to your original posture. This falling practice is also effective in strengthening the muscles of your neck, back, and stomach.

①   ②   ③

ZENPO KAITEN UKEMI 前方回転受け身
Forward Roll

① Stand with your right foot forward. Hold your right hand out in front of you, your elbow slightly bent, and your fingers straight but not spread. Hold your left hand down by your left hip, and as with your right hand keep your fingers close together, ready to slap the floor.

② Let your upper body fall forward. Make first contact with the floor with the back of your right hand near your little finger. Kick off from the floor with the toes of your right foot. Keep your left leg straight and swing your left foot up and over in a large circle. Keep your chin in, and your back rounded.

③ Roll forward over your right arm and rounded back, making contact with the floor with your right wrist, elbow, shoulder, and then your back in that order. Keep your chin in close to your chest so that your head does not hit the floor. When rolling over do not close your eyes.

④⑤ When rolling, keep your left leg straight and your right leg bent at the knee, so that your right foot comes down vertically onto the floor. Before your feet hit the floor, slap the floor with your left hand in order to lessen the impact on your feet. Press down with your right foot, and make contact with the floor with the outside of your left foot, so that your body is leaning diagonally forward to your left. Use the momentum of your forward roll and lift your head up to stand up in one smooth motion.

① ② ③

④ ⑤

Gozo Shioda, applying the
Second Control to force two
opponents into submission.

WAZA NI HAIRU DOSA 技に入る動作
Opening Attacking Moves

For all basic Aikido throws, the throw starts with a certain attacking move—for example, a strike to the forehead, a strike to the side of the head, or a punch to the chest. The methods of striking, punching, and countering these attacks are fixed, and are to be followed precisely. In striving to improve your techniques, you and your opponent must practice these moves faithfully without neglecting any of the steps.

SHOMEN UCHI 正面打ち
Strike to the Forehead

①② Stand with your right foot forward. Raise both hands over your head in preparation to strike at your opponent's forehead. Make sure that you do not lift your shoulders and that you keep your elbows in.

③④ Keeping your back straight, strike (chop) at the middle of your opponent's forehead with the side of your right hand, sliding forward at the same time as you strike.

① ②

③ ④

SHOMEN UCHI NO UKEKATA 正面打ちの受け方
Countering a Strike to the Forehead

①② Stand facing your opponent, left foot forward. Your opponent stands right foot forward. Your opponent slides forward on his front foot and strikes (chops) at your forehead with the side of his right hand. When your opponent raises his hands over his head in preparation to strike, raise your own hands over your head.

③ Meet your opponent's strike with the side of your right wrist, and as you make contact, thrust the fleshy inside of your wrist forward, deflecting the momentum of your opponent's hand. Bring your left hand up to your opponent's right elbow. Keep your weight firmly over your front foot.

①

②

③

YOKOMEN UCHI　横面打ち
Strike to the Side of the Head

① From the Basic Stance, right foot forward, raise both hands up over your head.

② Sliding forward on your front foot, cut down diagonally with your right hand. As you cut down, turn your hips to the right, so that the strike is not simply just a swing of your hand.

①

②

YOKOMEN UCHI NO UKEKATA　横面打ちの受け方
Countering a Strike to the Side of the Head

① From the Basic Stance, left foot forward, raise your hands up over your head as your opponent raises his hands.

② As your opponent strikes at the side of your head, slide your left foot diagonally forward to the left, blocking your opponent's strike with the side of your left wrist. At the same time, aim a back-handed punch at your opponent's face with your right hand. As you block your opponent's strike with your left wrist, thrust the inside of your left wrist forward to deflect the momentum of your opponent's right hand to the outside.

①

②

SHOMEN TSUKI 正面突き
Punch to the Chest

① Stand in the Basic Stance, right foot forward.

② Slide your right foot back behind you, and draw your right fist back to your side, ready to punch.

③ Thrusting forward with your hips, take a large sliding step forward with your right foot, and punch at your opponent's stomach.

④ Put your weight firmly on your right foot, with your right knee bent, pushing your hips even further forward. At the same time slide your back (left) foot up so that the spacing between your feet does not become too wide. Keep your left leg straight.

①   ②   ③   ④

SHOMEN TSUKI NO UKE-NAGASHIKATA 正面突きの受け流し方
Deflecting a Punch to the Chest

① Stand facing your opponent, left foot forward. Your opponent stands right foot forward.

② As your opponent slides his back foot behind him and prepares to punch, slide forward one step on your front (left) foot to keep the distance between you the same.

③ As your opponent punches, pivot on your front (left) foot, rotating your back (right) foot around clockwise behind you. Make contact with your opponent's right wrist with the side of your left hand to deflect his punch to the right.

①   ②   ③

RIDATSU-HO 離脱法
The Method of Freeing your Hand from a Wrist Grasp

① Your opponent grasps your wrist firmly and pushes.

②③④⑤ Use your opponent's push to pivot on your front foot, as in Body Movement Exercise Type 2, allowing your opponent's momentum to carry him forward, swinging your hand around palm up to destabilize your opponent's posture. Turn your hand back over in a scooping, circular movement, and slide your wrist out from between your opponent's thumb and forefinger.

①

②

③

④

⑤

October 1980. Demonstration tour in North America. Immediately after Gozo Shioda, focusing his strength in his finger, pokes his opponent in the throat.

USHIRO WAZA HOJO DOSA 後ろ技補助動作

Preparatory Exercise for Throws Where Your Opponent Attacks from Behind

① You and your opponent stand facing each other, right foot forward.

②③ Your opponent strikes at your forehead with the side of his right hand. Block the blow with the side of your right wrist, and draw your left hand back to your side in a fist in preparation to punch at your opponent's stomach.

④⑤⑥ Punch at your opponent's stomach with your left hand. Your opponent cuts your right arm down with his right wrist, and then slides past you on your right-hand side to come around behind you. (If you are in the Left-Handed Basic Stance, your opponent will slide past you on your left-hand side.)

⑦ Your opponent stands behind you, right foot forward. In the case shown here, your opponent attacks by grasping both your wrists.

①

②

③

④

⑤

⑥

⑦

A FINAL NOTE

It is my belief that all people are born with inherent individual natural talents. In my case, being born with an Aikido Master for a father, I have been immersed in the world of Aikido since I was small. In that environment, it was easy for me to lose sight of who I was, and I wanted to escape into the outside world. I became more and more self-centered and my Aikido techniques suffered as a result. However, as years have passed, I have come to understand that being meek has led to me losing my ego.

In order to discover the natural abilities within us, it is essential to remain meek, and to strive to lose our egos. With this humility, if you devote yourself wholeheartedly to one thing, strangely enough, those around you will come to support you in your efforts. I feel that Aikido is the method of finding this humility. It is a long road, but if you train with the perseverance to make steady progress, this opportunity will surely open up to you. Learn to unite your body and your feelings, do not forget your original sense of purpose, attempt to lose your ego and you will surely find the hidden talents within you. I would be delighted if this text served as a guidebook to this end.

Yasuhisa Shioda

Gozo Shioda and Yasuhisa Shioda.

Demonstration during the Tsukudo Era.
(When the Dojo was at Tsukudo Hachiman)

A scene of Gozo Shioda teaching at the Tsukudo Hachiman Dojo.

THE NAMES OF AIKIDO THROWS

The names of Aikido moves can be broken down into three parts. The first part of the name describes the way in which you are attacked. The second part is the Aikido technique you use to "defeat" your opponent. Thus "Wrist Grasp; First Control" means that the move starts when your opponent grabs your wrist, and you use the "First Control" technique to subdue him.

The third part of the name refers to "Type." There are almost always 2 types of each basic throw. Type 1 is generally where you are pulled, and move forward to apply a technique. Type 2 is generally where you are pushed, and spin or turn first, before overcoming your opponent.

TERMINOLOGY

Rotating (Spinning)

This refers to the technique of pivoting on one foot, and bringing the other foot around, either clockwise or anti-clockwise, in a curve.

Turning

This refers to the technique where your feet do not move, but your upper body turns to face the opposite direction.

Toes bent up

Keeping your toes bent up under you means that you are pushing down on the floor with your toes, your feet are perpendicular to the floor, and your buttocks are on your heels.

Toes flat down

When your toes are down, the backs of your toes are flat on the floor, and your buttocks rest on the soles of your feet.

Contact information for the author is as follows:
WEBSITE: www.yoshinkan.jp/indexE.html
E-MAIL: baba@yoshinkan.jp